Early Medieval Hagiography

PAST IMPERFECT

Overviews of the latest research by the world's leading scholars. Subjects cross the full range of fields in the period ca. 400–1500 CE which, in a European context, is known as the Middle Ages. Anyone interested in this period will be enthralled and enlightened by these overviews, written in provocative but accessible language. These affordable paperbacks prove that the era still retains a powerful resonance and impact throughout the world today.

Early Medieval Hagiography

James T. Palmer

ARC HUMANITIES PRESS

British Library Cataloguing in Publication Data
A catalogue record for this book is available from the British Library.

ISBN (print): 9781641890885
eISBN (PDF): 9781641890892
eISBN (EPUB): 9781641890908

arc-humanities.org
Printed and bound by CPI Group (UK) Ltd, Croydon, CR0 4YY

Contents

Contents

For Justine

Acknowledgements

The present book has been brewing in different forms for a number of years. It began in 2011 with a series of lectures on the cults of saints presented in Oslo at the invitation of Jón Viðar Sigurðsson—a generous host—as part of an Erasmus teaching exchange. Other projects then overtook me. In 2015, Erin Dailey kindly reached out to see if I would be interested in writing a volume on hagiography for Past Imperfect. Happily, shortly afterwards, I was invited by Jay Rubenstein and Tom Burman—more generous hosts!—to become the Lindsay Young Visiting Senior Scholar at the MARCO Institute, University of Tennessee, Knoxville, during part of the spring of 2016. Much progress was made possible. My school and the Dean's Office at the University of St. Andrews generously released me from teaching and prodeaning that semester to work on the book. Somehow, I was able to continue writing on my return, and I need to thank Justine Firnhaber-Baker and Alex Woolf in particular for helping to keep things ticking along to the end intellectually. Audrey, Sophie, and Hayden were also inspirational sources of endless energy. I would also like to thank Erin, Simon Forde, and Ruth Kennedy at Arc Humanities Press for their work in bringing the book to publication, and the two reviewers for the Press for applying their critical eyes to the project.

Introduction

Books about saints have an enduring appeal. In many ways, saints are heroes in the commonly understood sense. Most went on adventures or faced some kind of adversity, and therefore people looked to them in admiration and for inspiration. Saints could be ordinary people who worked hard to achieve standards few others could reach, and people looked up to them for that. Sometimes they were more otherworldly: outsiders, or the unimaginably rich, or the unimaginably poor. Stories about saints capture the imagination and many have become a staple part of modern culture—St. Patrick ridding Ireland of snakes, St. George fighting the dragon. Saints' stories even form part of the long-standing Penguin Classics series, making them from one perspective part of the modern literary canon of world culture. The stories tell of saintly and heroic ideals, but these are always shaped by the ways in which the stories are told, the way the author and audience relate to each other, and expectations about what a good hero/saint should do. Indeed, the hero/saint themselves, even a reluctant one, usually knows what is expected of them in these stories and is able to take on specific predetermined roles as necessary. The boundaries between stories and real life are not especially strong in that sense, because it is natural for people to interpret their experiences as stories or parts of stories.

The saint as exemplar, the saint as embodiment of story, is a fascinatingly ubiquitous phenomenon—a fact that should open up rich worlds for understanding hagiography that go beyond the familiar Western canon.[1] Buddhism in India had a variety of figures portrayed for emulation or devotion, including the Buddha, the pratyekabuddha, the arhant, and the bodhisattva.[2] The tradition of venerating holy men was strong in Buddhist Tibet, too, where Padmasambhava, the eighth-century founder of the monastery of Samye, was popular; and a significant tradition of *Nathar* developed, revealing enlightenment through example. Biographies about holy men can be found in Japan, such as the various stories that circulated about the Buddhist priest Gyōki (d. 749). Hinduism also had its iconic figures, such as Adi Shankara (d. 820, or possibly over a millennium earlier), who founded monasteries and wrote commentaries on Hindu sacred texts. In Islam, there were revered figures who attracted biographical treatment, starting with the *Sīra* about the Prophet and extending to other inspirational figures such as the learned jurist al-Shāfi'ī (d. 820). Jewish traditions, too, have a kind of holy man with the *tzadik*, a particularly righteous individual, even if there are no saints per se. Western Christian traditions are often studied without reference to such things but, in our globalized world, a more global perspective is often needed—and, in fact, it helps to sharpen our investigations to see the ways in which common, timeless concepts of religious cultural heroes were developed to meet specific local contexts.

The present book represents a playful attempt to capture the nature of saints' stories in the early medieval West while attempting to identify some ways forward for a more global, comparative approach in future. It aims to consider what hagiographies specifically reveal about European history during and after the fading of the Roman Empire in the Latin world that other sources do not. In doing so, I want to try to highlight the diversity and complexity of the period, rather than to reduce things to simple stereotypes or typologies. (As this is a short book, I warn you I will not always be successful.) Biographical or historiographical stories about saints—i.e., hagiography in the commonly understood sense—were a near-universal way of framing the past and society at a local level. Communities rallying around towns or monasteries, from Ireland to Syria and beyond, revelled in accounts of the efforts of people who founded their worlds, who defined their place in an always-evolving Christendom, who transcended normal things to become closer to God. Hagiography provided something of a common cultural resource alongside religious texts and the calendar, but one which lent itself to endless adaptation to fit local tastes, circumstances, and political needs. Indeed, many stories found expression in different ways in language, too, from Syriac to Old Irish, even if my expertise means that I will tend to focus on Latin texts from across the West. There were, of course, ritualized settings for encountering the stories—read out or retold during church services, or during feasts, or while on pilgrimage—all occasions when choice of language and register might be important. These tales often fed back into further stories, as people wanted to know about the posthumous power of the saint. If one wanted to understand the many varied experiences of the early Middle Ages across time and space, hagiography would offer an unrivalled source-type—always familiar, and yet so often distinctive.

For comparisons to be meaningful, there need to be appropriate guiding principles. There is no point comparing two things that have no conceptual or structural common ground, especially if they are significantly removed from each other in time and space. A useful rule of thumb is provided by Chris Wickham, reflecting on the insights of Carlo Ginzberg: "[I]f we want to compare across different societies, a good way to do it is by taking *spie* [spyholes] which are sufficiently similar in each society that they are comparable [...] but which articulate with the other elements of each society in different ways."[3] Hagiography from Europe to China provides such "spyholes" because it involves similar ideals and literary structures, articulated in response to different political, social, cultural, or religious circumstances. One can argue productively about whether to privilege similarities or differences, and whether either are more apparent than real. Without a sense of the questions to be addressed and the reasons for comparison, one is at best left looking for patterns in randomly generated data while relying on unreflexive aesthetic judgements.

The widespread use of hagiography in early medieval Europe is striking because Europe was not culturally homogeneous in every way. If one surveyed the region around 500 CE, one would find a number of relatively new kingdoms emerging, some rooted in the institutions and ideals of the Latin Roman world, others less so. Christianity and its hagiographical traditions had only recently arrived in Ireland and had yet to arrive in the English kingdoms, much of Germania, Scandinavia, and northeastern Europe. While Christianity introduced many common points of reference, including many "universal saints" such as the apostles, there were many debates ongoing about Christ's nature, the use of relics and images, and penitential practice—so much debate, in fact, that Europe's Christian communities adhered to a disparate array of practices and beliefs. Fast forward to around 900 and one will not find much less variety: many practices and beliefs had changed, sometimes considerably. Christianity in the north now stretched far beyond the old Roman frontiers of the Rhine and the Danube, creating new heroes in its wake, but it also had a far-diminished presence in the Near East, North Africa, and Iberia because of the Arab conquests and the spread of Islam—two distinct processes—in the seventh and eighth centuries. Many of those nascent kingdoms from the fifth century had collapsed, some spectacularly, and the powerful empires people experienced were now those of the Franks and of the Byzantine world. And everywhere people wrote, circulated, and read hagiography as they reflected on the ever-shifting relationship between their specific circumstances and the universal religion to which they belonged.

An important part of shifting circumstances in the West was a change in how people were connected to the eastern parts of the Mediterranean. The sixth century witnessed a decisive consolidation of imperial authority in Byzantium as the West fragmented. Justinian's effort to re-establish direct imperial rule in the West between the 530s and 560s failed abysmally, despite strong support for the principle of empire in areas of Italy, Iberia, and Gaul. Trade and travel persisted, but the patterns changed.[4] East-West cultural exchange, facilitated by the great translators such as Evagrius (d. 399) and Jerome (d. 420), slowed. Command of Greek in some western areas may have gone into terminal decline, but we should also remember that Latin itself was moving into areas where it was a distinctly foreign language while also evolving into new vernacular forms in Italy and Gaul.[5] For hagiography, these and other factors reinforced regional variation and a decline in the East-West exchange of stories about saints.[6] New traditions began to emerge slowly, at least in Old Irish and Old English. For all this, however, Latin hagiographic culture maintained its connections with older Eastern traditions. Indeed, hagiography offers one accessible way to explore East and West in comparison, as traditions with similar core DNA evolved to fit new circumstances and occasionally met up again later.

We need to ask how hagiography reflected all this change. Often, the contours of saints' ideals and struggles reveal much about the values of the society which created her or him, particularly in the way that people might be expected to look up to the hero as a figure to imitate. Hagiographies tell us about sex, marriage, charity, struggles with poverty and wealth, government and corruption, outsiders to the community, and attitudes towards nature and the miraculous, to pick out just a few common topics. Many authors portrayed these issues through accounts of conflict, with saints resisting secular social roles, chastizing sinners, or facing hostility from people who did not share their ideals. But while saints, male and female, had tendencies to act in set ways, the worlds they interacted with could be wildly different. One could flee to the desert, as St. Anthony did in the story written by Athanasius of Alexandria and translated by Evagrius of Antioch, but one might have to contend elsewhere with a metaphorical desert—a remote island for St. Cuthbert of Lindisfarne in northern Britain, or a forest for Sturm, founder of Fulda in Germany. One also needed to be realistic: one pious individual in sixth-century Trier who wished to imitate the famous "pillar saints" of Syria was literally brought down to earth by his bishop because it was too cold in northern Europe for such behaviour (Gregory of Tours, *Histories*, bk. 8, chap. 15). Standards of sanctity were always adapted to their cultural and environmental settings.

At the same time, the stories are fundamentally about conflict—how the hero stood out from the crowd; how they challenged or were challenged by norms, practices, institutions, and people. The classic holy woman or man gained their power from the margins, from the desert, from the renunciation of the sex or wealth or gluttony of everyday life.[7] Few heroes are ever minted by blandly behaving like everybody else. We might like heroes or celebrities who are in some sense just like us, but by definition they aren't: there always has to be something about them—some deed, some ability—which sets them apart in a way which makes them hard to imitate. As Peter Brown once noted about the kind of saints we will encounter in this book, the true heroes could not be too easy to imitate, otherwise becoming a hero would be too easy and the distance between sacred and profane would quickly collapse.[8] In Byzantium (and indeed Buddhist China), different traditions even emphasized hidden sanctity, partly to promote humility, but also to restrict access to the holiness. Saintly heroes were by definition exceptional.

It is not just action and behaviour that matters here but, more explicitly, charisma. In the classical model adapted from Max Weber's sketch about compelling political leaders, the saintly hero might be an individual whose personal authority moulds and directs a group of followers to such an extent that the group may fall apart without them.[9] The leader does not have to be "charismatic" in the modern sense of someone charming and magnetic, although no doubt that often helped. Charisma could be "routinized" and ultimately transferred to institutions (such as monasteries or churches), where it would become part of a different kind of long-term institutionalized authority through practices of memory and identity. Hagiographers wrote both to promote and to routinize charisma for our saintly heroes, so their work can reveal much about strategies for generating and maintaining power in a range of circumstances. Often, crucially, this charisma coincided with patterns of social status and values.[10]

Discussion of charisma as discourse of power leads to another crucial reason why we are so interested in these old sacred biographies: we are perpetually fascinated by what makes people do things. Some earlier generations were not so interested in this with regards to hagiography and saints' cults, as they viewed the whole thing as the worst of uncultured, popularist, superstitious nonsense.[11] Power, to such sceptics, is anything but those things: it is often exclusive and grounded in the nation state or government, law, war, and money. But in practice we increasingly appreciate that it is rarely just a matter of hierarchy and force. People respond to rhetoric and performance, to stories, to education, to the habits and ideals of their social environment, in ways that are not always planned or limited to those who think they are in control. Wars in Vietnam and Iraq were fought for "hearts and minds," not just bodies and infrastructure. Elections are won by tabloid rumour and lost by body language regardless of political ability. Sex and looking the part matter even when they shouldn't. Saints as semi-marginal figures are interesting in these contexts because of the ways in which they inspired action through good examples, charity, and powerful words, despite not always having the best material backing or social platforms, but by almost always having the best publicity. Indeed, hagiography inspired action by keeping the examples of the saints going, and not a little by distorting the past and offering subjective—sometimes overtly propagandist—views on kings, bishops, and social practices. Hagiography should not be underestimated: it did not just reflect political discourse, but was part of it. Kings and aristocrats read or heard the stories of the saints, and some even played an active role in writing them out.

One of the central reasons why modern historians are interested in hagiography is that it provides evidence about women, non-elite people, and anyone that chronicles, letters, laws, and other sources simply do not cover. To give but one example: from the Roman *gesta martyrum* (Deeds of the Martyrs) we can find out much about late-antique households, changing gender expectations, and family dynamics, which are at best only hinted at elsewhere.[12] Yet just because there is evidence for something does not always mean that people will value or analyse that evidence. The baggage of people not taking hagiography seriously in the past still weighs heavily today. That has changed profoundly with the development of gender studies, "history from below," and the study of the relationship between ideas, society, and action in various configurations of literary, cultural, and praxis histories. We will explore the dynamics involved here more fully in Chapter 3 on "Historians and the Quest for Truth." We need to remember that how we approach hagiography as a historical source is always bound up in our present concerns. As Benedetto Croce proposed, "ogni vera storia è storia contemporanea"—"all true history is contemporary history."[13]

We have proceeded so far without defining what hagiography is beyond vaguely noting that it tends to be the story about an inspirational individual—that is, a kind of biography. This vagueness is partly a deliberate move, because the definition of hagiography has proven rather controversial. Where once the Bollandist Hippolyte Delehaye, writing *Legends of the Saints* in 1905, could confidently write about biographies that aimed at edification and pertained to a cult, by the early 1990s there was less certainty about either of those things. Should one include writings about saints that were not biographies? What did it even mean to say that hagiography is a genre or a type of source if so many writers subverted generic expectations? Would talking about "hagiography" in the early Middle Ages have been meaningful given that there was no single comparable term in use, and is it meaningful to us now? Are there better terms, like the "sacred biography" Thomas Heffernan suggested in his 1988 book of the same title to avoid the baggage of "hagiography"?

And what happens to our definitions when we start to consider non-European, non-Christian "biographies about holy people" if they aren't tied to the ideas about sanctity that drove traditions of scholarship?

A central concern is whether hagiography is really distinct from other historical writings. A hard separation of the two will not do, especially if what one is talking about is a distinction between fanciful hagiographies and the "hard facts" of chronicles.[14] Such distinctions can be illusory, not least because we often find ourselves trying to impose modern definitions and abstractions on medieval material. At the most sceptical end of the spectrum, such concerns led Felice Lifshitz to declare:[15]

> The concept of a genre of "hagiography" is a historiographical construction and, *ipso facto*, an ideological tool. It is a tool that had no function in the ninth, tenth, and eleventh centuries, and thus as a conceptual category it did not exist. It should not be anachronistically applied in our analyses of [in her example] late Carolingian and early Capetian Franca, because it can only obscure the realities of those centuries, not illuminate them.

Reflecting on this argument in 2013, Anna Taylor conceded that the term "hagiography" is too useful to abandon completely, and that many medieval writers did perceive connections between their works.[16] Many historians working on Latin and Greek traditions have preferred Marc Van Uytfanghe's idea of "hagiographical discourse" defined by four features: the focus on a subject close to God; the stories' subjectivity, often rooted in oral traditions; the emphasis on idealization, apology, and edification over being informative; and a tendency to see the world in fixed terms revolving around stock themes.[17] It is a bit looser than "genre," may be more appropriate for non-Christian texts, and may also encourage people to examine texts about saints that go beyond "sacred biographies," such as sermons or letters.

Arguing about definitions of hagiography, much like arguing about definitions of "the Middle Ages," does not necessarily get us very far. One is still left with plenty of texts written about saints, many written generically, and many for which there were medieval "conceptual categories" such as *vitae* (Lives), *passiones* (Sufferings), or *miraculae* (Miracles). There was no "one size fits all" approach to any aspect of a saint's story or any related theological, liturgical, or performative aspects. As a historian, it is still what you do with any given text that matters. Labels such as "hagiography" are often best used as jumping-off points for analysis rather than end points. They should certainly not be used as a substitute for critically evaluating each text on its own merits. Not, alas, that that is always what happens.

In the meantime, there have been a good number of projects aimed at helping people to get a sense of written dossiers about saints in various forms. A significant number of texts are edited in some form in one or both of the Bollandists' *Acta Sanctorum* and the volumes of the Monumenta Germaniae Historica, now both navigable digitally. The Bollandists also contributed significantly to the disentangling of different texts by introducing the *Bibliotheca Hagiographica Latina*, *Graeca*, and *Orientalis*, which assigned BHL, BHG, or BHO numbers to each one—also now searchable online. For a grand survey of hagiographies across time and space, one should consult the multi-author, multi-volume *Corpus Christianorum Hagiographies* series, started in 1994 by Guy Philippart and still incomplete, which divides the vast field by time and place. For Gaul, more detail on sources can be found in the scattered contributions to the project "Les sources hagiographiques narratives composées en Gaule avant l'an mil (SHG)," initially driven by François Dolbeau, Martin Heinzelmann, and Joseph-Claude Poulin. Walter Berschin discussed many saints' Lives in his magisterial analysis of the evolution of biographical forms ca. 300 to ca. 1220, *Biographie und Epochenstil im lateinischen Mittelalter*, taking the first three volumes (of five) to cover the chronological range the present little book does. For Byzantine hagiography, there is now the exemplary two-volume *Ashgate Research Companion to Byzantine Hagiography* (2011-2014), edited by Stephanos Efthymiadis, with essays covering many aspects of what made hagiography in the East work.

The shape of the present book is designed to take readers from the creation of medieval hagiography, through the ways in which it circulated, to the different strategies used by historians and literary scholars over the past century or so to interrogate the sources. Such a structure highlights the inevitable processes by which stories acquire new meanings, first as they told or imagined, then as they are written down, then as they are copied or edited or read, and then, with time, as people removed from the initial world of composition engage with the story for new purposes. Chapter 1 examines how hagiographers created saints, working with memories, literary traditions, and outright imagination to create something useful for authors and audiences to pursue their specific agendas. Chapter 2 turns to the world of hagiography after composition to ask how texts circulated, what associations between texts emerged, and how other kinds of sources—calendars, sermons—reframed the original logic of hagiographical stories. Hagiographers may have had all sorts of plans for their compositions, but often had little control over how their texts were actually used. With the medieval world of hagiography sketched out, the second half of the book turns to the modern use of those texts. Chapter 3 provides a potted history of the scholarly study of hagiographies since the nineteenth century, with the intention of identifying strategies for using them and understanding some of the personal and intellectual politics, and heroes and anti-heroes, that have guided people in their work. The final chapter then sketches out some of the ways in which studying hagiography has made a difference to our understanding of the period 500-900.

A Note on References to Sources

In keeping with the mission statements of the Past Imperfect series, I have kept references to a minimum. For primary sources, I have often given book and/or chapter numbers (e.g., bk. 4, chap. 3), which refer to sections in the standard editions. What are the standard editions? Most standard Latin texts cited can be found edited by the Monumenta Germaniae Historica, in the French *Sources Chrétiennes*, or the Bollandists' *Acta Sanctorum* series. I have included some major collections of texts in translation in the Further Reading section, and these too will direct you to the standard editions. If the text or edition is a bit more obscure, I have added further details in an endnote. Most endnotes contain references to essential secondary literature, which, of course, is also useful for identifying editions.

Notes

[1] See the essays in *Sainthood: Its Manifestations in World Religions*, ed. Richard Kieckhefer and George D. Bond (Berkeley: University of California Press, 1988).

[2] Reginald Ray, *Buddhist Saints in India: A Study in Buddhist Values and Orientations* (Oxford: Oxford University Press, 1994).

[3] Chris Wickham, "Problems in Doing Comparative History," in *Challenging the Boundaries of Medieval History*, ed. Patricia Skinner (Turnhout: Brepols, 2009), 5–28 at 13.

[4] Michael McCormick, *The Origins of the European Economy: Communications and Commerce AD300–AD900* (Cambridge: Cambridge University Press, 2001).

[5] Walter Berschin, *Greek Letters and the Latin Middle Ages: From Jerome to Nicholas of Cusa*, trans. Jerold Frakes (Washington, DC: Catholic University of America Press, 1988); James Adams, *The Regional Diversification of Latin 200BC–AD600* (Cambridge: Cambridge University Press, 2007) and his *Social Variation and Latin Language* (Cambridge: Cambridge University Press, 2012).

[6] Claudia Rapp, "Hagiography and Monastic Literature between Greek East and Latin West in Late Antiquity," in *Christianità d'occidente e cristianità d'oriente*, Settimane di studio della Fondazione

centro italiano di studi sull'alto medioevo 51 (Spoleto, Centro italiano di studi sull'alto medioevo, 2004), 1221–80.

[7] Peter Brown, "The Rise and Function of the Holy Man in Late Antiquity," *Journal of Roman Studies* 61 (1971): 80–101; reprinted in his *Society and the Holy in Late Antiquity* (Berkeley: University of California Press, 1982), 103–52. Claudia Rapp, "Saints and Holy Men," in *The Cambridge History of Christianity* 2, ed. Augustine Casiday and Frederick Norris (Cambridge: Cambridge University Press, 2008), 548–66; *The Cult of Saints in Late Antiquity and the Early Middle Ages*, ed. Paul Hayward and James Howard-Johnston (Oxford: Oxford University Press, 1999), esp. the essay by Averil Cameron.

[8] Peter Brown, "Enjoying the Saints in Late Antiquity," *Early Medieval Europe* 9 (2000): 1–24 at 16–17.

[9] Albrecht Diem, "Monks, Kings, and the Transformation of Sanctity: Jonas of Bobbio and the End of the Holy Man," *Speculum* 82 (2007): 521–59.

[10] Friedrich Prinz, *Frühes Mönchtum im Frankenreich: Kultur und Gesellschaft in Gallien, den Rheinlanden und Bayern am Beispiel der monastischen Entwicklung, 4. bis 8. Jahrhundert* (Vienna: Oldenbourg, 1965); Martin Heinzelmann, "Neue Aspekte der biographischen und hagiographischen Literatur in der lateinischen Welt (1.-6. Jahrhundert)," *Francia* 1 (1973): 27–44.

[11] In different ways, this negative attitude inspired both Hippolyte Delehaye, *Les légendes hagiographiques* (Brussels: Société des Bollandistes, 1905); trans. Donald Attwater, *The Legends of the Saints*, 4th ed. (Dublin: Four Courts Press, 1998), and Peter Brown, *The Cult of the Saints: Its Rise and Function in Latin Christendom* (Chicago: Chicago University Press, 1981).

[12] Kate Cooper, *The Fall of the Roman Household* (Cambridge: Cambridge University Press, 2007); *Religion, Dynasty, and Patronage in Early Christian Rome, 300–900*, ed. Kate Cooper and Julia Hillner (Cambridge: Cambridge University Press, 2007), especially the central trilogy of essays by Sessa, Jones, and Leyser.

[13] Benedetto Croce, *Teoria della storiografia* (Bari: Gius, Laterza & Figli, 1920), 4.

[14] Baudouin de Gaiffier, "Hagiographie et Historiographie. Examen de quelques problèmes," in *La storiografia altomedievale*, Settimane di studio del Centro italiano di studi sull'alto medioevo 17 (Spoleto: Centro italiano di studi sull'alto medioevo, 1970), 158–59; Friedrich Lotter, "Methodisches zur Gewinnung historischer Erkenntnisse

aus hagiographischen Quellen," *Historische Zeitschrift* 229 (1979): 298–356 at 308; Jean-Michel Picard, "Bede, Adomnán, and the Writing of History," *Peritia* 3 (1984): 50–70.

[15] Felice Lifshitz, "Beyond Positivism and Genre: 'Hagiographical' Texts as Historical Narrative," *Viator* 25 (1994): 95–113.

[16] Anna Taylor, "Hagiography and Early Medieval History," *Religion Compass* 7 (2013): 1–14.

[17] Marc Van Uytfanghe, "L'hagiographie: un 'genre' chrétien ou antique tardif?," *Analecta Bollandiana* 111 (1993): 135–88. Martin Hinterberger, "Byzantine Hagiography and its Literary Genres: Some Critical Observations," in *Ashgate Research Companion to Byzantine Hagiography* 2 (Aldershot: Ashgate, 2014), 25–60.

Chapter 1

Making Saints (Up)

Any study of hagiography must start with more or less the same question: what were people who wrote stories about saints trying to achieve? If one looks at samples from across early medieval Europe, one could be struck both by how creative hagiographers could be, and how conservative they could be with their themes and motifs. One might note with surprise that writers from Ireland to Rome wrote about similar ideas of purity and sin using similar textual role models, such as St. Martin of Tours, the fourth-century soldier-turned-hermit-turned-bishop, or St. Benedict of Nursia, the sixth-century abbot and founder of monasteries; and just as often one might note the significant differences in worldview and context suggested by the same texts. All hagiographers started, in some sense, by wanting to do something with the story of a particular saintly hero—to celebrate their achievements, obviously, but maybe also to make particular moral, theological, or political points. We start, therefore, by exploring some of the different factors that shaped the process of producing hagiography. To do so takes us to the heart of how individuals and communities described their world in text.

A useful and amusing example is provided by the eighth-century failed saint Aldebert of Soisson (cited in the Letters of Boniface, no. 59). Aldebert knew all about how to make a saint. People dedicated churches to saints and distributed their relics. They told stories about their heroic piety, drawn from books. In life, saints were usually marked by a piety which challenged the norms of the time, and there were signs that proved their sanctity. Understanding the game, Aldebert set about establishing himself as a real, living saint. He encouraged people to set up oratories near their fields; he told them they did not need to confess their sins to obtain salvation; he told them they did not need to travel to Rome on pilgrimage—all things which made salvation more accessible to ordinary people than they were through the institutional Church. He distributed his own hair and fingernails as sacred objects. And, perhaps most importantly of all, he wrote his own saintly biography, the *Life of Aldebert*, which started with a vision his mother had had during pregnancy foretelling his sanctity. Aldebert tried to make himself into a saint and knew what he was doing.

In many respects, Aldebert played fair. There was no official process of canonization when he lived in the eighth century—that was still centuries away.[1] All you needed to be recognized as a saint was for someone to recognize you as a saint. There were, of course, standards, but these were not hard rules. Miracles were entirely optional, especially between the eighth and tenth centuries when there was a widespread aversion to overusing stories of the subversion of the laws of nature to promote faith.[2] But you did have to have lived a good life at some point, and it was easier for all concerned if some aspect or aspects of your behaviour seemed comparable to what recognized saints might do. Having sex and children, or even participating in war, did not necessarily rule you out if your audience believed you had other things in your favour, maybe a late-blossoming austerity, or the fact that you had once been generous to a monastery. We shall see many examples in this chapter. All you needed was for people to believe; or, preferably, to have someone write a convincing account of you at some point.

Unfortunately for Aldebert, his behaviour jarred horribly with the prevailing official mood in his native Gaul and beyond.[3] He was roundly condemned by bishops and nobles led by Pippin III—father of the famous emperor Charlemagne (d. 814)—at a council in Soissons in 744. Then, for good measure, his case was discussed at a second council in Rome in 745, where he was condemned for a second time. A leading bishop from the north sent a dossier of materials to the Roman meeting to aid with Aldebert's condemnation, and it included the *Life of Aldebert*. To play by the rules properly in the West, a saint should be dead before he could be proclaimed a saint. (This was not always so clear-cut elsewhere.) The northern bishop dramatically called Aldebert "a precursor of Antichrist." Pope Zacharias denounced "blasphemers and schismatics" such as Aldebert, and praised Pippin and his bishops for maintaining a sense of order.

The lead bishop in the north also knew the unwritten rules of the game. St. Boniface was Archbishop of the Germans and had had a long and distinguished career, first as a teacher in his native Wessex, then as a missionary in Frisia, and finally as a reformer in the lands east of the Rhine between his base in Mainz and the Thuringian Basin.[4] Boniface was not the name he had been born with: originally called Wynfreth, he symbolically assumed a new name in Rome on the day of his ordination to match that of one of the old martyrs from one of the great Roman persecutions of Christians. He read and collected hagiographical stories. He challenged lax standards in the Church, proselytized to pagans, and founded or helped to found a number of churches and monasteries in Germany. Not for him the anti-institutional mindset Aldebert had set out. And when he died in 754—murdered in Frisia by pagan pirates, possibly outraged by his actions, but also possibly just after his wine—he was quickly proclaimed a true martyr and saint by his friends and acquaintances. His body was retrieved and buried in the monastery of Fulda in Germany, and local aristocrats rushed to grant new lands to the centre in the martyr's honour. After a couple of years, a biography of the saint was produced which praised his heroic and timeless piety—and which naturally gave space to condemning Aldebert in the process.

The contrasting stories of Aldebert and Boniface highlight many of the crucial issues involved in the making of saints in the early Middle Ages. In another time and another place, Aldebert could have been the success story.[5] Indeed, just over a century earlier, in Burgundy, the superstar saint *par excellence* was a radical Irish holy man named Columbanus, whose actions took monastic spaces out of the control of kings and Gallo-Roman bishops; unpopular with the powers-that-were, keen to agitate for new standards, he was no institutional figure playing by the old rules. But Columbanus, unlike Aldebert but like Boniface, shaped the zeitgeist and was lucky enough that his friends and patrons retrospectively controlled the discourse on who the real heroes of the age were. Around 640, Jonas of Bobbio wrote a *Life of Columbanus and his Companions*, a significant work which played at a number of levels. Jonas claimed to be writing in the orthodox spirit of Athanasius, author of the *Life of Anthony*; St. Jerome; and the authors of various "recollections" (*memoriae*) about St. Martin of Tours (bk. 1, chap. 1). He omitted or distorted various stories about Columbanus to make him appear less controversial. The exception here was the saint's struggles against the royal line of Brunhild, which were worth celebrating in 640 because the rival royal line which had defeated Brunhild's in 613 were themselves now in trouble and needed support. Jonas talked up Columbanus's connections with noble families who now dominated the political scene, such as St. Audoin of Rouen's.[6] He also sought to defend the legal position of the Columbanian monasteries and to portray those in charge of them as the spiritual heirs of the holy man even though, as seems likely, they actually held different values. Jonas may have relayed many stories which reflected "what had actually happened," but the telling of those stories was a highly complex piece of social and political argumentation. He who controls the past may well attempt to shape the future with it.

The rest of the chapter seeks to sketch out some of the strategies and habits that lay behind the composition of saints' stories in the early medieval West. This necessarily covers a variety of issues concerning literary form, the politics and mechanisms of memory, the political life of the saint and her or his followers, and changing cultural values. I will not attempt to be exhaustive by any stretch, but I will hopefully illustrate some of the key issues involved in the creation of hagiography.

Writing Saints' Lives: Texts and Memories

The creation of a saint depended on the productive and unpredictable meetings of life and text. The foundations of thinking about sanctity had roots which predated Christianity, particularly in Jewish traditions about persecuted prophets and in Greek and Roman stories about heroes overcoming adversity. Stories such as the murder of Eleazar from 4 Maccabees prefigured discussions of Christian martyrdom. Christ himself provided a rich example of how someone could provide spiritual leadership with moderation and the occasional miracle—an example which was developed significantly in the stories about the apostles. *Imitatio Christi* was important and shaped the stories and language of post-biblical hagiographies, from the early *Martyrdom of Polycarp* onwards. Christ's words, miracles, and sufferings were those of the saints.

But sanctity was necessarily something more than a matter of someone embodying the virtues discussed in the Bible. There was no vision for an institutional Church during Christ's ministry, nor for monastic discipline, because the end of the world was expected soon. When the world did not end (again and again), people modified the ideals of leadership in response to the new types of activities they pursued, from the creation of bishops, abbots, and abbesses onwards. Moreover, defining shocks came with the persecution of Christians and the creation of martyrs, particularly those during the Diocletian persecutions of ca. 303, whose fearless deaths provided inspiring testimony of God's power. There may have been a timeless core of saintly ideals; changing circumstances, however, ensured that those ideals were added to or developed over time, or simply came to mean something different than originally intended.

One reflection of the growing variety of sanctity is the emergence of different types of hagiographical text. The standard form most people today expect is the biographical narrative (*vita*, Life), although many such texts are built around episodes rather than in strict chronological progression. Some texts focus on the suffering and death of the saint (*passio*, Suffering) and some on the legal trials involved (*acta*). The importance of relics to a cult meant that stories might involve the dramatic discovery of the saint's body (*inventio*), tales of miraculous healings and other events at a shrine (*miracula*), or the process of moving a saint's body from one location to another (*translatio*). There were no strict rules about any of this and many legends developed organically, so a single text might contain all of the above elements or even none depending on what the author was attempting to do, what their subject had done, and what the audience believed or wanted. In addition to these common kinds of hagiography, there are a wide range of texts which intersect with saintly traditions. People discussed saints in letters and, of course, engaged in epistolary communication with them if they were still alive.[7] Homilies, which provided material for preaching, could be relevant too. Calendars, martyrologies, and litanies provided liturgical settings for understanding saints. Hagiographies only ever provided snapshots of traditions about saints which otherwise continued to evolve in response to changes in memorial and liturgical practice and in response to political and polemical need.

One of the most striking features about hagiographical texts is how quickly they became generic. Among the earliest stories produced in Rome about martyrs, there are a good number which contain vivid contemporary details or which betray concerns about orthodoxy that help to date them, such as those composed during the Laurentian Schism in the years around 500.[8] The problem then, of course, is that people who wanted to promote their saint or cause looked at the successful saints' stories and copied the best ideas—particularly if their saint was long-dead and semi-legendary anyway. That much is natural. The result could be the imaginative expansion of literary borders. It could, however, also end up with the production of bland stories about saints who were just like other saints—sometimes to the extent that the stories were virtually the same, only with the names and a few key details changed. Importantly, this is more of a problem for modern historians and critics than it was for people writing hagiography in the sixth century, as the intention of many hagiographers was indeed to make their subject as much like a generic saint as possible. To muddy the waters further, many people who became saints knew that they were behaving in the spirit of these semi-literary creations, and so their actual lives may already have deliberately had a rather generic air to them as they imitated their role models. Audoin of Rouen, for instance, was reportedly self-consciously austere at the court of Dagobert I (d. 639), according to the *Chronicle of Fredegar* (chap. 78)—something that does not seem surprising when one reads his *Life of Eligius of Noyon* and discovers that he was very familiar with the examples of saints written about by Rufinus, Jerome, and Sulpicius Severus. If you are dealing with stories that are supposed to inspire people, you have to be prepared for the distinction between fiction and reality to be rather murky as ideas and ideals affect real-life behaviour.

Implicit in the above discussion is a crucial point: people valued the literary nature of hagiographies as well as their theological and historical contents. It may be subjectively true that few hagiographies stand up as well-crafted literary creations. Nevertheless, a major factor in the production of hagiography alongside the need to commemorate a saint was the desire to rewrite texts to improve them. All three of Alcuin of York's (d. 804) extant hagiographies, about Vedastus (St. Vaast, d. ca. 540), Richarius (St. Riquier, d. 645), and Willibrord (d. 739), were about long-dead saints subject to earlier accounts, the first two in a difficult Merovingian Latin and the third in a now-lost Insular Latin, none of which Alcuin felt were stylistically appropriate for audiences by the late eighth century.[9] Alcuin was the first person to discuss "correcting" Latin, but his fellow countryman Bede had already led the way with his improved *Life of Cuthbert* (ca. 720), developing an anonymous earlier text—"if better means more classical, grammatical, antiquarian," Walter Berchin remarked dryly.[10] Before even Bede, Cogitosus of Kildare, working around 680, had improved passages from the *First Life of Brigit* while otherwise lobbying for the importance of Kildare as a centre of the Church in Ireland.[11] Also in the seventh century, Leontius of Neapolis supplemented Sophronius's *Life of John the Almsgiver* so that Sophronius's lofty style could be complemented with more directly accessible stories. The practice of "metaphrasis"—paraphrasing or improving the text rhetorically—was a big part of eastern hagiographical tradition.[12] Style mattered.

The way memory was practised played a crucial role in the shaping of much hagiography too.[13] Memory can be a slippery thing—loose and unsystematic at both the level of the individual and the collective. Memories can be forgotten or become associated with ideas or events with which they originally had no connection. Moreover, memory often required practice through discussion, ritual, or text in order to make it present, often in relation to specific places. Hagiography developed multiple functions in relation to these practices. Stories were often the result of someone collecting stories and giving them a coherent form on which people could more or less agree. Reading and listening also helped people to remember the saints and their stories, whether or not they had known them and whenever and whereever they lived.

First-hand knowledge gave many hagiographies their authority. Texts in the East, from the fourth-century *History of the Monks in Egypt* to John Moschos's *Spiritual Meadow* in the seventh century, were grounded in the authority of people witnessing real-life holy behaviour.[14] Part of the success and power of Sulpicius's *Life of Martin* was that Sulpicius as an author knew his subject personally (as he reminds the reader throughout).[15] Such proximity could lead to a vividness that raised a text above mere cliché, as in Stephanus of Ripon's tales of the persecution of serial fugitive St. Wilfrid of York, or

Audoin of Rouen's reflections on the piety and goldsmithery of his friend Eligius of Noyon.[16] If the author's authority as witness was not sufficient, further eyewitnesses could supply testimony. Several stories in the anonymous Lindisfarne *Life of Cuthbert* were supplied by named individuals—the priest Tydi (bk. 2, chaps. 4–5; bk. 4, chap. 6), the anchorite Hereberht (bk. 4, chap. 9), the abbess Aelflaed (bk. 4, chap. 10). In Iberia, the author of the *Life of Fructosus of Braga* not only appealed to the miracle stories told by the priest Benenatus that proved their hero's sanctity, but also recorded them as Benenatus's direct speech to underscore the point. Leontius of Neapolis, too, reported stories from the church treasurer Menas about John the Almsgiver. Audiences were not the gullible consumers of stories some people today assume: hagiographers needed to give them reasons to believe and to make the stories memorable.

Often the recollections seem already to have had a story-like form. Sulpicius told of a time when the devil pretended to be the Second Coming of Christ to trick Martin, but Martin would not be fooled and the devil fled. He then added, "this event, as I have just related, took place in the way that I have stated, and my information regarding it was derived from the lips of Martin himself; therefore let no one regard it as fabulous" (bk. 1, chap. 24). The famous eighth-century account of Willibald's travels to the Holy Land was reportedly based on the saint's own testimony to the nun Hugeburc fifty years later, a feat of memory seemingly assisted by the saint's own written notes on his itinerary. Sometimes, it seems, written notes could be crucial. Another fifty years later, Rudolf of Fulda was entrusted with the composition of a life of the nun Leoba, a colleague of Willibald's. The account was expressly based on the testimony of four of her disciples, who each wrote down notes for posterity; they were then quizzed by a monk called Mago, who made his own notes here and there but who died without having the opportunity to turn them into something more coherent until they came into Rudolf's possession. In all of these cases, we can see the importance of chains of authority, legitimizing the truth claims of the hagiographer—but all of them rooted in the act of circulating and verifying stories.

Fears that memory might be eroded also encouraged attention to be paid to these chains of authority. Rudolf's contemporary Lupus of Ferrières discussed precisely this issue in his preface to the *Life of Wigbert of Fritzlar*. Writing in 836, he was aware that Wigbert had died ninety years previously, and sceptics might call his account into doubt. How could he really be said to know about the distant past? But he pre-empted such criticism by pointing out that Sallust and Livy had written about times before they had lived, as had Jerome with the *Life of Paul the Hermit* and (Pseudo-)Ambrose in his account of St. Agnes. He also sought to restrict himself to writing about events which could be found in other writings or, for more recent miracles, which he had been told by eyewitnesses. His contemporary, Ermanrich of Ellwangen, faced a much steeper challenge, as nobody knew anything concrete about his subject, St. Sualo, so he created a patchwork of spiritual truths and circumlocutions, offset by an eyewitness account of the translation of the saint's body.[17] Saints who were more legendary than historical were acceptable as long as they were presented correctly. A hagiographer needed to be able to position themselves carefully between the different traditions in circulation, lest they be accused of writing lies and fabrications. Hagiographers did not always have complete freedom to invent whatever they fancied, even if there was still significant freedom for artistic licence.

Early Irish examples highlight some of the same issues when there was an even greater length of time between the saint and the hagiographer. When Cogitosus wrote his *Life of Brigit of Kildare*, he was almost certainly writing at least a century after the events he described. He could, however, refer in his preface vaguely to information passed down from "well-informed elders," and it seems that he had access to other Lives of Brigit, perhaps including the *First Life*. Certainly Donatus of Fiesole (d. 876) knew of two old Lives which are no longer extant. Adomnán of Iona, writing about St. Columba around 697, also referred to stories "either from among those things that we have been able to find put into writing before our time, or else from among those that we have learned, after diligent inquiry, by hearing them from the lips of certain informed and trustworthy aged men who related them without any hesitation" (Adomnán, *Life of Columba*, Pref.). Here again, in yet another corner of Christian Europe, the production of a hagiographical text evolved in relation to a living body of stories, oral and written, each with a different authoritative status depending on how they were preserved.

The difficulty, as is well known, is how fluid memory can be in the face of forgetfulness, institutional change, and political expediency. Sometimes what you do not say is crucial. Competition between the churches of Autun and Poitiers over the body of St. Leudegar (d. ca. 679) led to the production of two versions of essentially the same text, telling of political intrigue, betrayal, and murder, except the Autun version did not mention explicitly what happened to the body while the Poitiers version did (they had it). Jonas of Bobbio conveniently forgot to mention that Burgundian bishops had once branded St. Columbanus a heretic, no doubt as part of a strategy to present Columbanus's political and cultural sensibilities as being more in tune with those of his successors. The *Life of Queen Balthild* fails to mention anything about the number of bishops she was supposed to have ordered to be executed, although it does include a curious circumlocution to explain her subsequent retirement from public life ("And from this a dispute arose because [some nobles] killed [Sigobrand] against her wishes. Fearing that the Lady would hold it gravely against them and wish to vindicate his cause, they straightaway permitted her to go into the monastery [of Chelles]" (chap. 10). Exactly what she wanted in the circumstances, no doubt). All of which is to say that, while collective memories could limit creativity in some respects, the process of lobbying for an agreed version of the past sometimes led to authors being strategic in what they recalled and how. This, as we shall see next, is often where the politics comes in.

The Politics of Saints

The desire to memorialize saints in particular ways often points towards the political dimensions of saint creation. Often, this was an extension of controversies during the saint's life. St. Wilfrid provides something of an extreme example: Stephanus moved quickly to write after his bishop's death, because Wilfrid's controversial career had seen him and his followers chased into exile from Northumbria more than once, and without their charismatic leader, his heirs looked vulnerable to further persecution. In Maastricht, around the same time, a priest was quick to write an account of Bishop Lambert (d. 705), who had also spent time exiled from his see, but who was murdered in revenge for the death of two boys connected to the household of Duke Pippin II (d. 714), a figure who at the time was developing something of a stranglehold on Merovingian politics (chaps. 11–12). Saints needed to be defended from the controversies of their lives, not just for the sake of posterity, but also for the benefit of those who stood to gain or lose from subsequent discussion of what had happened.

Orthodoxy was often useful to the workings of "defensive hagiography." Sulpicius's St. Martin nearly died from eating hellebore, hiding from the persecution of Arian heretics (ca. 6). Gregory the Great's (d. 604) *Dialogues on the Italian Fathers* provided a catalogue of saintly behaviours to illustrate the posthumous powers of saints and their active afterlives in response to scepticism around the Mediterranean world all the way to Constantinople.[18] In Byzantium, the long-running debates over the use of icons in Christian worship generated many texts that celebrated saints and the theological issues they had represented. A good example is Stephen the Deacon's 809 account of Stephen the Younger (d. 765), which provides lively overviews of the debate in the course of condemning the evil Constantine V's persecution of the hero saint.[19] Because saints embodied "truth," people found it useful to employ them as part of their arguments about other issues.

Claims to more earthly things such as jurisdiction often determined claims about past and future. Cogitosus's *Life of Brigit* provided a bold example when the author claimed that Kildare was "the head of almost all the Irish Church with supremacy over all the monasteries of the Irish, and its *paruchia* extends over the whole land of Ireland, reaching from sea to sea" (Pref.). Here is a claim which would have raised a few eyebrows in St. Patrick-promoting Armagh, at least. Similar surprise may have followed Stephanus repeating Wilfrid's grand claim to speak "for all the northern parts of the islands of Britain and Hibernia, which are inhabited by the English and British as well as the Scots and Picts" at a synod in Rome in 680 (chap. 54). Not every claim to authority was necessarily so explicit or expansive, as is illustrated by the case of the *Life of Willehad* and the *Life of Liudger of Münster*, both written around 843 and both containing claims that it was *their* saint who had evangelized lands along the fluid Saxon–Frisian frontier.[20] Needless to say, jurisdiction over the lands in question were disputed at the time as three Carolingian kings divided territories between them. One might doubt that hagiographies were the only tool employed to establish control over particular lands; stories, however, ultimately supported any legal claims to be made at councils or court.

Writing about saints could be part of high politics too. King Sisebut of the Visigoths (d. 621) wrote a *Life of Desiderius of Vienne* which has been interpreted as an effort to celebrate the downfall of the Merovingian line of Brunhild, herself originally from the Iberian peninsula. Whether such a text was expected to fulfil a diplomatic purpose, building bridges between the Visigoths and Franks, one can sadly only speculate, as there is no hard evidence concerning Sisebut's intended audience.[21] Sisebut at least had good company in criticizing Brunhild's line as this was a central plot device in Jonas of Bobbio's work, too, as we saw above. Not that contemporaries were slow to criticize controversial members of the triumphant branch of the family, King Dagobert I (d. 639), King Childeric II (d. 675), and Queen Balthild. Such stories could represent political partisanship, just as they could in Ireland, England, or anywhere else. Sometimes hagiographers wanted to demonstrate the gravitas of their saint by showing them "speaking truth to power" in the manner of Old Testament prophets.

Setting Standards

The negotiability of standards for sanctity could open up some unusual situations. If the process of arguing for someone's sanctity was more liberal before canonization, what happened if people were prepared to proclaim someone unsavoury a saint? In the twelfth century, Guibert of Nogent could still grumble that Bretons venerated St. Piro (or Pyr), the sixth-century Welsh abbot who died, drunk, falling into a well.[22] But what if the problem was more straightforward, such as a change in what was considered socially acceptable in terms of saintly or aristocratic behaviour? Or what if the whole point of the saint's success was that she or he challenged these standards?

Many saints' Lives certainly provided useful "rule books" for behaviour. It has long been recognized that the point of a saint is that they are a role model, an exemplar, somebody whose piety, charity, and continence anyone might aspire to match. Texts were explicitly designed to carry such exemplars of behaviour, from the works of Gregory of Tours to the sixth-century Chinese *Biqiuni Zhuan* ("Lives of the Nuns").[23] Preferably, of course, the example should be sufficiently hard to imitate that not everyone could hope to reach the standards of saints.[24] Sometimes the examples could be highly specific. Talk about a monastic "rule of Columbanus" is best understood as referring to the examples of monastic behaviour set out in Jonas's *Life*, albeit, as Anne-Marie Helvétius has stressed, with implications for the reform of society more generally.[25] Agius of Corvey, writing around 876, explicitly stated at the end of his *Life of Hathumoda of Gandersheim* that he hoped the stories of Hathumoda's self-control and generosity would act as a rule for the nuns of her house, strengthened by the emotional bond of remembering. Many texts acted as narrative endorsements of experimentation with a variety of monastic practices, for instance for Benedict Biscop in Jarrow or Philibert in Jouarre in the seventh century. Some could be more critical, such as Eigil of Fulda's critique of the emphases placed on different practices in his own monastery or Ardo's mockery of Benedict of Aniane's early experimentations with extreme asceticism (if the whole thing isn't a twelfth-century concoction anyway). Stories made different theories of behaviour active and so open to assessment.

The sex lives of saints provided particularly uneven terrain. Chastity was, of course, greatly valued, but it was never a necessary condition for sanctity in the period. One of the most popular early martyrs was St. Perpetua, who was a married noblewoman forced to give birth in prison while waiting to be killed at the games.[26] A significant ingredient in her popularity was the human tragedy of her story—that Perpetua was just a normal person, persecuted for her faith. Saints' stories needed to offer some realistic social context. In seventh-century Gaul, Bishop Arnulf of Metz, Queen Balthild, and Sadalberga were each afforded the status of saint, each having had children within the legitimate confines of marriage. This happened with Theodora of Thessaloniki in the 890s, too. Understanding limits was important. Sadalberga was said to have desired taking religious vows, "if sex had not been an impediment and royal snares not entrapped her" (*Life of Sadalberga*, chap. 9). But what were the limits? The story of Mary of Egypt proved popular in East and West: Mary was a sexaholic prostitute who sought to increase her number of sexual partners by going on pilgrimage to Jerusalem, only to be overcome with remorse for her sins there before retiring to the wilderness as a hermit. There was usually space for the truly penitent—just not always.

A particularly complex attitude towards purity is demonstrated by Aldhelm of Malmesbury's (d. 709) *On Virginity*, which created a catalogue of saintly examples to inspire the nuns of Barking. Aldhelm argued that purity was fundamentally a matter of discipline. Virginity was useless to someone if it was the only virtue they could observe. Indeed, if it is a matter of discipline and mind, why deny equivalent status to women who had once been married with virtue and now lived as a nun with virtue? The reality of life had to temper the standards one hoped people could achieve. Nevertheless, Aldhelm then summarized the sufferings of the great saintly heroes, from Old Testament prophets, via confessors such as Martin and Benedict, to the great virgin martyrs such as Cecilia and Agnes of Rome, and Agatha and Lucia of Sicily, who all preferred the sword to the defilement of their bodies. In essence, Aldhelm was doing little more than paraphrasing the core virtues and achievements of the saints from the standard, much as Bede would do in more perfunctory style in his martyrology (see Chapter 2). What is interesting for us is to see the active appropriation of these examples to offer inspiration to a particular audience on a specific theme.

The idealization of virginity remained important. Bridget of Kildare allegedly avoided marriage by gouging out her own eye, according to the ninth-century *Bethu Brigde* (chap. 15). Northumbrians venerated Balthild's contemporary Queen Æthelthryth (d. 679) precisely because she maintained her virginity despite being married twice. St. Wilfrid even claimed to Bede to have proof of her virginity, just in case anyone was unsure (Bede, *Ecclesiastical History*, bk. 4, chap. 19). According to Stephanus, Wilfrid himself had once refused a marriage offer and vast tracts of land in Lyon to pursue his spiritual calling, highlighting that these were crucial issues for men too (chap. 4). Yes, there may be temptation, but there was nothing discipline could not solve. Gregory's St. Benedict was once troubled by remembering a woman he had seen once, so he tossed himself into a thorn bush (*Dialogues*, bk. 2, chap. 2). The aristocratic saint Gerald of Aurillac was nearly undone when, as a young man, he visited a girl whose skin immediately caught his attention; but God intervened by making her repulsively ugly later on and Gerald's chastity was miraculously preserved (bk. 1, chap. 9). Gerald might have counted himself lucky as few people were helped out of their own lust.

The sex lives of ordinary people offered further challenges and opportunities. Sex tainted everything. The source of Columbanus's conflict with Theuderic II was that he did not approve of the king having concubines instead of a legally recognized wife (bk. 1, chap. 18). A woman in Saxony caused St. Liudger of Münster great distress, according to Altfrid, because she wanted to give some honey to his company, but he recognized that the gift was corrupted by the fact that she had taken an unlawful husband (bk. 1, chap. 28).[27] In both of these instances the saint corrected the behaviour of the people they met. And so it went. Few saints went as far as St. Emmeram of Regensburg, who was "martyred" after voluntarily taking the blame for getting a local nobleman's daughter pregnant, while the girl and her lover escaped her father's wrath. Symeon the Fool, however, flirted with prostitutes and even refused to deny getting a slave girl pregnant, so that people would not guess that he was a saint.[28] One almost wonders at times where saintly values end and satire starts.

Shifting standards of sanctity meant that even a martyr's death could be open to interpretation, too, as Emmeram's case might suggest. In truth, dying for the faith had always been controversial; it became particularly problematic once Christians were not a persecuted minority but the baggage of being persecuted never truly went away. Gregory of Tours, in his *Glory of the Martyrs* (chap. 106), was by no means unusual in directing his readers to think about martyrdom in terms of struggle rather than spectacular and elaborate murder. There was interest in blood martyrs in Ireland, England, and Spain, but it remains striking that no major biographical product from these regions was dedicated to one other than martyrologies (see Chapter 2). In Gaul, things proved more complex. On the one hand, there was a growing literature which tied the great Gallic dioceses to martyrs who, in the telling, sounded much like the famous persecuted martyrs of Rome and the East—figures such as Dionysius of Paris or Crispin and Crispinian of Soissons. On the other, there was a cluster of seventh-century episcopal figures—Leudegar of Autun, Praejectus of Volvic, Lambert of Maastricht—who were discussed as martyrs, even though their murders were the results of feuds and high politics. This last trend played to the common desire to make a hero out of a victim, but it soon led to increased regulation of how someone was recognized as a saint under the Carolingians.[29] In response, the ninth-century West witnessed a significant shift in emphasis towards the celebration of old martyrs and confessors, with a corresponding growth in accounts of shrine miracles and accounts of transferring relics to new sites.[30] A new kind of writing about relic translations developed, inspired by Einhard's account of his acquisition of Ss. Peter and Marcellinus.[31] What people valued in a saint, and why, was subject to fashion and canon law.

In the same way, one might often wonder about tastes concerning the miraculous. The ninth-century author of the *Second Life of Boniface* in Utrecht took time to defend his writing from critics who did not appreciate the lack of miracles in his tale. Signs and prodigies, he countered, were only for the weak of faith (chap. 14). Indeed, this was not an age in which hagiographers revelled in writing about wild miracles. The vast majority of stories are healing miracles: people regaining sight or mobility after praying at a shrine. Many played on the virtue of providential coincidence, such as the time Cuthbert was hungry and found some food in a shepherd's hut (anonymous *Life of Cuthbert*, bk. 1, chap. 6 or Bede's version, chap. 5). On the whole, hagiographers did not display a disregard for the laws of nature, no doubt to ensure their stories were believable. Cainnech of Agahboe (d. ca. 600) even refused to allow God to move a mountain for him in Scotland when his light was blocked (*Life of Cainnech*, chap. 21).[32] What Cainnech really wanted, according to his hagiographer at least, was inner discipline. Not every audience was credulous and nobody could really hope to move mountains through prayer, but every audience turned to the stories of the saints at least for inner discipline.

Hagiography, Study, and Performance

How, then, did audiences encounter saints' stories to get these messages? Most modern discussions of the issue are obliged to refer to Alcuin of York's (d. 804) preface to the *Life of Willibrord*, written for the monastery of Echternach near Trier. Most prefaces to hagiography—if indeed there is one—stress the modesty of the author and the historicity of the saint. Alcuin, however, outlined why he had written two versions, one in prose and one in metre. (Apart from Bede's treatment of Cuthbert, it was not usual to produce two together.) The first, he suggested, was ideal for reading out to edify monks in church. The rare poetic account, on the other hand, he thought lent itself better to private study and reflection. Form and function were closely linked. Of course, Alcuin's imagined audience was basically the same for both texts: a monastic one that could deal with Latin. Not all audiences for such texts were cloistered, we can be sure, and many texts were for both readers and listeners (Leontius's *Life of Symeon the Fool* refers to both). The use of hagiography no doubt contained some variation.[33] As suggested previously, there were lively oral cultures surrounding the telling of saints' stories, often with exchanges at churches or saints' feasts. These exchanges covered a wide spectrum of society, including religious and lay people.

A central issue for engaging audiences in the West was language.[34] Most of the extant early medieval hagiography from there was written in Latin. At the beginning of our period Latin was not a dead language, only for use in intellectual circles, but a living, breathing, and regionally diverse language for many. If someone had read out the Latin *Suffering of St Sernin* in a church in Toulouse in the fifth century, people would have understood it. But Latin separated as a spoken and as a written language, with the consequence that it is likely fewer uneducated people could understand it by the time of Charlemagne. In the meantime, the Latin of many saints' Lives from seventh-century Gaul may have seemed odd and often ungrammatical—"barbaric," in the opinion of editors at the Monumenta Germaniae Historica (see Chapter 3)—but that may say more about linguistic change and nineteenth-century gentlemen than Merovingian educational standards. Reformers such as Alcuin insisted on asserting better standards of written Latin in the eighth century, inspired by the Roman classics, and hagiography started to become less accessible outside a more limited ecclesiastical hierarchy—unless preachers regularly read out hagiographies in off-the-cuff translations.

The composition of hagiography in many areas evolved where there was no gradual separation of spoken and written Latin. Many speakers of Old Irish and of Germanic languages may only have encountered Latin as an artificial medium for church ritual and learned endeavour. In an odd story in Willibald's *Life of Boniface*, the Englishman is presented as so anxious about speaking Latin to Pope Gregory II that he insisted on writing his confession of faith down, presumably in order to avoid any grammatical slips that would have resulted in accusations of heresy (chap. 6). It highlights, nevertheless, a distance between written and spoken language and capabilities in both. Unsurprisingly, in Ireland and the English kingdoms this soon led to a culture of writing vernacular hagiographies, presumably to make key texts accessible. Many early texts in both traditions are largely translations, such as the *Bethu Brigte*; but there is plenty of evidence of cultural adaptation, too, such as in the Old English *Andreas*'s poetic retelling of St. Andrew as hero. For Western Europe as a whole, however, the composition of hagiographies in the vernacular remained highly unusual.

Translation into Latin was still important for making texts accessible in other contexts. The liveliness of East-West exchanges of hagiographical material may have slowed from the seventh century, but there remained active routes, particularly via Italy. Bede knew, and indeed revised, a translation of the *Suffering of Anastasius the Persian*, about a seventh-century martyr killed by Zoroastrian Persians at St. Saba's, the story having possibly been transmitted to Britain by Theodore of Canterbury, who had fled Cilicia in Asia Minor in his youth before being directed north by Pope Vitalian (d. 672).[35] The greatest programme of translation was undertaken by Anastasius Bibliotecarius in ninth-century Italy, including Leontius's *Life of John the Almsgiver* (for Pope Nicholas I), Sophronius's *Miracles of Cyrus and John*, and parts of John Moschos's *Spiritual Meadows*.[36] Anastasius wanted to make Greek texts available in Latin, but he chose examples that highlighted the struggle of the Church and the authority of Rome—even directing an account of the military saint Demetrios of Thessaloniki to King Charles the Bald (d. 877) to emphasize the point.[37] An interesting issue here, crucial for Chapter 2, is that few of the Eastern saints were probably subject to any active cult in the West. Bede and Anastasius may have hoped that such cults would develop. It is more likely, however, that people enjoyed and benefited from saints' stories regardless of cultic context. For all their differences, for all their cultural repackaging, most saints still ended up looking and sounding like someone who could be understood as a saint anywhere.

Conclusion: Writing Hagiography

What, then, were the writers of hagiography trying to achieve? We have seen a range of examples of people working between literary and oral traditions, or between lived experience and social memory. People shaped their stories to reflect theological and cultural preferences. They composed texts for reading, for reading out loud, for making stories accessible, and as literature. Some people were interested in themselves or their friends as saints, and some people were more interested in people long dead. The problem with early medieval hagiography is that there was always an exception and there are no hard rules, making rash generalizations fragile. But people did do a lot of thinking about and thinking with the saints. Literature about the saints created a space in which ideals about religion, gender, power, or society could be explored in non-abstract ways.

To end, it may be worth having a (non-exhaustive) handlist of common reasons given for why people wrote hagiographies:

- to promote the cult of a recently deceased holy person
- to promote the cult of a long-dead holy person
- to explain why a saint's relics are in a certain place
- to justify recent actions by a particular group (political or religious)
- to assert a community's authority in a certain region (might involve legal documents)
- to counter or complement claims made in other hagiographies
- to provide a displaced autobiography
- to provide examples of good and bad behaviour (including examples of canon law in action)
- to encourage missionary work in a particular area
- to create a sense of local identity
- to provide edificatory readings for church services and monastic mealtimes
- to provide an authoritative version of past events where there are competing traditions (written or oral)
- to associate a particular saint with dynastic propaganda
- to broker between cultures
- to improve upon existing literary products
- to update the cultural sensibilities of existing literary products.

Notes

[1] André Vauchez, *Sainthood in the Later Middle Ages* (Cambridge: Cambridge University Press, 1997).

[2] Marc Van Uytfanghe, "La controverse biblique et patristique autour du miracle, et ses repercussions sur l'hagiographie dans l'antiquité tardive et le haut Moyen Âge," in *Hagiographie, cultures et sociétés, IVe–XIIe siècles* (Paris: Études Augustiniennes, 1981), 205–33.

[3] For a useful account of Aldebert's opponents' concerns see Sven Meeder, "Boniface and the Irish Heresy of Clemens," *Church History* 80 (2011): 251–80.

[4] The most recent studies are James T. Palmer, *Anglo-Saxons in a Frankish World 690–900* (Turnhout: Brepols, 2009) and John-Henry Clay, *In the Shadow of Death: Boniface and the Conversion of Hessia 721–54* (Turnhout: Brepols, 2010).

[5] Matthew Innes, "Immune from Heresy: Defining the Boundaries of Carolingian Christianity," in *Frankland: Essays for Dame Janet Nelson*, ed. Paul Fouracre and David Ganz (Manchester: Manchester University Press, 2008), 111–35.

[6] Yaniv Fox, *Power and Religion in Merovingian Gaul: Columbanian Monasticism and the Frankish Elites* (Cambridge: Cambridge University Press, 2014). For the text, see now Alexander O'Hara and Ian Wood, *Jonas of Bobbio: Life of Columbanus, Life of John of Réomé and Life of Vedast* (Liverpool: Liverpool University Press, 2017).

[7] Claudia Rapp, " 'For Next to God, You Are My Salvation': Reflections on the Rise of the Holy Man in Late Antiquity," in *The Cult of Saints in Late Antiquity and the Early Middle Ages*, ed. Paul Hayward and James Howard-Johnston (Oxford: Oxford University Press, 1999), 63–82.

[8] See the survey by Cécile Lanéry in *Hagiographies* 5, ed. Guy Phillipart (Turnhout: Brepols, 2010).

[9] Christiane Veyrard-Cosme, "Alcuin et la réecriture hagiographique: d'un programme avoué d'*emendatio* à son actualisation," in *La réécriture hagiographique dans l'Occident medieval*, ed. Monique Goullet and Martin Heinzelmann (Ostfildern: Thorbecke, 2003), 71–86.

[10] Walter Berschin, "*Opus deliberatum ac perfectum*: Why Did Bede Write a Second Prose Life of Cuthbert?," in *St Cuthbert, His Cult and His Community to AD 1200*, ed. Gerald Bonner, Clare

Stancliffe, and David Rollason (Woodbridge: Boydell, 1987), 95–102 at 97.

[11] Richard Sharpe, "*Vitae S. Brigidae*: The Oldest Texts," *Peritia* 1 (1982): 81–106, but note the argument that Cogitosus's work precedes the *Vita prima* in Kim McCone, "Brigit in the Seventh Century: A Saint with Three Lives?," *Peritia* 1 (1982): 107–45.

[12] Daria Resh, "Towards a Byzantine Definition of Metaphrasis," *Greek, Roman, and Byzantine Studies* 55 (2015): 754–87.

[13] Catherine Cubitt, "Memory and Narrative in the Cult of Early Anglo-Saxon Saints," in *The Uses of the Past in the Early Middle Ages*, ed. Yitzhak Hen and Matthew Innes (Cambridge: Cambridge University Press, 2000), 29–66.

[14] Georgia Frank, *The Memory of the Eyes: Pilgrims to Living Saints in Late Antiquity* (Berkeley: University of California Press, 2000).

[15] Clare Stancliffe, *St Martin and his Hagiographer: History and Miracle in Sulpicius Severus* (Oxford: Clarendon Press, 1983).

[16] Paul Fouracre, "Merovingian History and Merovingian Hagiography," *Past & Present* 127 (1990): 3–38.

[17] Lynda Coon, "Historical Fact and Exegetical Fiction in the Carolingian Vita s. Sualonis," *Church History* 72 (2003): 1–24.

[18] Matthew Dal Santo, *Debating the Saints' Cult in the Age of Gregory the Great* (Oxford: Oxford University Press, 2012).

[19] Marie-France Auzépy, *L'Hagiographie et l'Iconoclasme Byzantin: le cas de la Vie d'Étienne le Jeune* (Aldershot: Ashgate, 1999), building on her edition and translation of the text in the same series two years earlier.

[20] Palmer, *Anglo-Saxons in a Frankish World*, 172–76.

[21] Jacques Fontaine, "King Sisebut's *Vita Desiderii* and the Political Function of Visigothic Hagiography," in *Visigothic Spain: New Approaches*, ed. Edward James (Oxford: Clarendon Press, 1980), 93–130.

[22] This is the starting story for Julia Smith, "Oral and Written: Saints, Miracles, and Relics in Brittany, c. 850–1250," *Speculum* 65 (1990): 309–43.

[23] Kathryn Ann Tsai, *Lives of the Nuns: Biographies of Chinese Buddhist Nuns from the Fourth to Sixth Centuries* (Honolulu: University of Hawai'i Press, 1994).

[24] Brown, "Enjoying the Saints in Late Antiquity."

[25] Anne-Marie Helvétius, "Hagiographie et réformes monastiques dans le monde franc du VIIe siècle," *Médiévales* 62 (2012): 33–48, esp. 40–41.

[26] Thomas Heffernan, *The Passion of Perpetua and Felicity* (Oxford: Oxford University Press, 2012).

[27] *Die Vitae Sancti Liudgeri*, ed. Wilhelm Diekamp (Münster: Theissing'schen Buchhandlung, 1881).

[28] Derek Krueger, *Symeon the Holy Fool: Leontius's Life and the Late Antique City* (Berkeley: University of California Press, 1996).

[29] Paul Fouracre, "The Origins of the Carolingian Attempt to Regulate the Cult of Saints," in *The Cult of Saints in Late Antiquity and the Middle Ages*, ed. James Howard-Johnston and Paul Antony Hayward (Oxford: Oxford University Press, 1999), 143–65.

[30] Julia Smith, "Old Saints, New Cults: Roman Relics in Carolingian Francia," in *Early Medieval Rome and the Christian West*, ed. Julia Smith (Leiden: Brill, 2000), 317–39.

[31] For context see Martin Heinzelmann, *Translationsberichte und andere Quellen des Reliquienkultes* (Turnhout: Brepols, 1979).

[32] The *Vita Cainnechi* is in *Vitae sanctorum Hiberniae*, ed. W. W. Heist (Brussels: Société des Bollandistes, 1965), 182–98.

[33] Katrien Heene, "Merovingian and Carolingian Hagiography: Continuity or Change in Public and Aims?," *Analecta Bollandiana* 107 (1989): 415–28.

[34] Marieke Van Acker, *Ut quique rustici et inlitterari hec audierint intellegant: hagiographie et communication verticale au temps des Mérovingiens (VIIe–VIIIe siècles)* (Turnhout: Brepols, 2007).

[35] Carmela Vircillo Franklin and Paul Meyvaert, "Has Bede's Version of the *Passio s. Anastasii* Come Down to Us in *BHL* 408?," *Analecta Bollandiana* 100 (1982): 373–400. On the archbishop's life: *Archbishop Theodore*, ed. Michael Lapidge (Cambridge: Cambridge University Press, 1995).

[36] Réka Forrai, *The Interpreter of the Popes: The Translation Project of Anastasius Bibliothecarius* (unpublished PhD dissertation, Central European University, 2008).

[37] Réka Forrai, "Byzantine Saints for Frankish Warriors: Anastasius Bibliothecarius' Latin Version of the *Passion* of Saint Demetrius of Thessaloniki," in *L'héritage Byzantin en Italie (VIIIe–XIIe siècle)* 3, ed. Sulamith Brodbeck, Jean-Marie Martin, Annick Peters-Custot, and Vivien Prigent. (Rome: École française de Rome, 2015), 187–202 (with the Latin text).

Chapter 2

Collecting Saints' Stories

The writing of sacred biography was only one part of the literary world of saints. Saints, hagiographers, and their audiences all knew that they were participating in a culture that transcended individuals to embrace the faithful collectively. That was the point of talking, as many did, about the Holy Church in the singular and talking about the collected fate of people on Judgement Day. For saints, it was crucial that at some level they had achieved their status because they had reached widely recognized standards, be they for virgins, anchorites, martyrs, or any other holy person. The power of the saint was also collective as they stood together as the elect of God, and indeed would form a particular group of the elect on Judgement Day. While the creation of a saint was often a local process, it was one which usually rested on near-universal standards built up from the exchange of stories, texts, and ideas over a long period of time and, sometimes, across great distances.[1] This raises important issues: how was knowledge about saints organized and how was it circulated?

Some of the central issues are laid out, conveniently, in a letter from Pope Gregory I to Bishop Eulogius of Alexandria written in around 598 (Letters, bk. 8, no. 28). We only have Gregory's part of the exchange, in which he states that Eulogius had requested "the deeds of the martyrs [*gesta martyrum*] which Eusebius of Caesarea of blessed memory had collected in the time of Constantine." The request surprised Gregory as he had never heard of the *gesta martryum* collected in this way, not by Eusebius, not in the papal archive, and not in the libraries of the city of Rome, "except for a certain few collected in a volume of a single manuscript." The only complete collection on the martyrs Gregory possessed, he noted, was in another book in which they were listed in liturgical order so they could be celebrated at Mass, but without any information on how they suffered; this kind of book, however, Gregory presumed Eulogius already possessed. We will return to the full implications of Gregory's letter a few times in this chapter. For now, it is necessary simply to bear in mind the possible modes of information exchange implied: through letters, through collections, through individual texts, through calendars (or, better, martyrologies), and through the liturgy.

Anyone who wishes to study the past through hagiographical material sidesteps issues of transmission and circulation at their peril. It was all very well that authors of hagiographies intended clever and subtle things with their narratives. But did the text reach its intended audience and have any effect? Did it unexpectedly influence different audiences? Was it copied or used widely, or was it just of local interest? Did interest in the saint change over time and, if so, did this generate new texts, either about the saint or about other saints? The afterlife of a text will not often tell us about authorial intention, but important study after important study has shown the importance of examining texts as they were developed in response to each other and to changing circumstances. Knowledge about saints spread through a variety of different channels, some textual, some oral.

From Intertextuality to Collections

Central to the issues at hand is the way that hagiographers responded to existing traditions. This is something that we have already encountered in Chapter 1 in some forms, but it is worth revisiting and expanding upon key issues. Fundamentally, a driving force in the production of early medieval hagiography was that each saint and each text was a new engagement with a larger part of a (notionally) single saintly tradition. Saints had role models and became role models; hagiographers had exemplars and their work became exemplary. Two of our lead hagiographers thus far, Jonas of Bobbio and Willibald of Mainz, opened their works by directly attempting to position themselves in relation to established classics of hagiography or church history. This is important: however one might try to define hagiography or sacred biography, it has to be recognized that people writing and using texts about saints saw them as somehow related, even if the texts produced were sometimes idiosyncratic.

The articulation of connections between saints can be suggestive here. One of the earliest Merovingian Lives, of Genovefa of Paris, included an implausible account of the Syrian ascetic Symeon Stylites (d. 459)—the famous pillar-hermit—being impressed at stories of her virtue (chap. 27). Maybe he was, for all we know, although few believe this. The purpose of the story, either way, was to authorize Genovefa's holiness by claiming the approval of a more established holy person, just as Symeon's appearances in the *Life of Daniel the Stylite* (ca. 500) had done at around the same time in the East. One can quickly assemble a list of similarly powerful guest appearances. Often these lent authority to proceedings, but they could also be competitive, as in the oddly grumpy appearance of Brendan in the Irish *Life of Ruadan* (chap. 3) or Columba in the *Life of Cainnech* (chap. 20), both of which seem designed to make a new saint look more measured than the more famous contemporary.[2] And while some of these little vignettes might have had a historical basis, we should remember that one of the things that made them compelling to audiences was a certain intertextuality—these were appearances by figures they had heard about in other stories.

Traditionally, the study of a saint's Life is exactly what it sounds like: the examination of a text about a pious individual. Many texts were not designed with such focus in mind. A foundational text here in more than one respect was Eusebius of Caesarea's *Ecclesiastical History*, which was translated into Latin and expanded by Rufinus of Aquileia

(d. 410). Eusebius sought to expand the narrative of the trials and tribulations of Christians from the time of the apostles to his own day. While this project involved more than writing about saints, Eusebius's work contained a significant catalogue of martyrs and other valiant heroes. Explicitly looking back at Eusebius's work and its pagan antecedents, Jerome composed his own catalogue of intellectual heroes, *On Illustrious Men* (written ca. 393). It may not have been strictly hagiographical either, but it identified men worthy of veneration and imitation, and it provided valuable inspiration and ammunition for Gregory of Tours, Isidore of Seville, and Bede in the West. In the East, meanwhile, writing about collections of saints flourished, notably with Cyril of Scythopolis's (d. 557) *Lives of the Monks of Palestine* (Greek, Chalcedonian) and John of Ephesus's (d. ca. 588) *Lives of the Eastern Saints* (Syrian, Monophysite).[3] Maybe it was a natural approach to take with the subject: in sixth-century southern China, in the region of Zhejiang, Hui Jiao compiled biographies of eminent Buddhist monks, too, that provided a model for future collections.[4]

Gregory of Tours' work represents one of the earliest hagiographical miscellanies of the early medieval West.[5] In a Jerome-imitating note at the end of his *Histories* (bk. 10, chap. 18), Gregory noted that he had written seven books of miracles and one on the *Life of the Fathers*; all of these we still have. There have been numerous theories put forward regarding the sequence and purpose of compositions, but the latest (which seems highly plausible) is this: that Gregory intended to issue them together as a single coherent collection but died before he had finished composing and editing them.[6] Given that some of the texts are themselves miscellanies about the miracles, the end result would have been a collection of collections of stories. These were wide-ranging texts: *Glory of the Martyrs* started with Christ and recited miracles concerning Mary and the apostles before discussing the power of early martyrs; *Glory of the Confessors* was no less eclectic in terms of stories told but did mostly focus on bishops, abbots, and other pious figures;

Life of the Fathers was comparatively biographical and more recent in focus; while books on the miracles of St. Martin of Tours and St. Julian of Brioude catalogued experiences of the miracles in Gallic society.

There are two features of Gregory's work of particular importance to the present study. First, there is his famous comment in the preface to *Life of the Fathers* that the singular *Life*, not the plural *Lives*, is preferable: "there is a diversity of merits and virtues among them, but the one life of the body sustains them all in the world" (Pref.). Saints are all on the same team. The second feature is the high level of intertextuality on show in Gregory's works. Gregory provided cross-references to relevant stories he had composed throughout both his hagiographical stories and *Histories*. He also related few biographical stories about saints because, in most cases, there existed texts such as the *Suffering of St Dionysius* or Sulpicius Severus's magisterial *Life of Martin of Tours* to do that for him. Gregory's hagiographical projects worked primarily because he expected that they would add to a tradition and body of knowledge, not because they would stand by themselves.

Interest in accumulating local traditions meant that people developed texts to provide a sequence of biographical sketches, often labelled *gesta* (deeds), often about bishops or abbots in a single institution. In some way the role model was the Roman *Liber pontificalis*, which provided accounts of varying length and emphasis for each pope up to the ninth century. Few historians would necessarily label it "hagiography" per se, especially when confronted with relatively dry lists of liturgical donations to churches around Rome. Still, it influenced the genre-bending late eighth-century *Deeds of the Bishops of Metz*, written by Paul the Deacon, which mixed potted accounts of episcopates, royal genealogy, and hagiographical episode to good effect in order to lay claim to Metz's importance among the Frankish churches.[7] Over the next two centuries a number of these were composed with understandably minimal circulation, as they built up a local institutional repository of memories—many, naturally, subject to the emphases and fancies of the polemicists who curated them.

It would be fair to say that, if one wanted a clear distinction between hagiography and historiography, one would not find it in the *gesta*. Bede composed a *History of the Abbots of Wearmouth-Jarrow* which, in its stories of Benedict Biscop, Ceolfrid, and others pursing a rigorous religious life while leading their monasteries, is not stylistically or thematically very different to his hagiographies. At the same time, in the way that Bede disentangled and explained the controversial recent history of the monastery, he also produced something which is more chronologically linear and less infused with the miraculous, more in keeping with his *Ecclesiastical History*. The same has been said of texts from John of Ephesus's *Lives of the Eastern Saints* to the *Deeds of the Bishops of Auxerre*, written in the ninth century, in the way they subvert modern expectations of hagiography. The boundaries between hagiography and history were at best impressionistic and dependent on many issues concerning the form and function of individual texts.

Manuscripts and Compiling Saints

Manuscript evidence for saints' Lives presents some different issues concerning how the stories of saints were related to each other. With no publishing industry, texts circulated copied by hand onto papyrus or treated animal skin, either as rolls or codices. This can make each copy of a text unique, possibly revealing something about the circumstances and purpose of its creation depending on how it was treated or what it was copied alongside. Manuscripts also remind us that there were physical and visual dimensions to these texts, with decisions about layout, calligraphy, and decoration that might convey something about the value or function of a text. Most of the examples in this book, including the legendaries, were modest in size (around 25 × 18 cm) and unillustrated but for some decorative titles and initials. This might suggest that they were, on the whole, practical products, although some were certainly executed with sufficient care to suggest higher-end usage.

The survival of manuscripts poses some problems and raises warnings. There is, for instance, only one Irish hagiographical manuscript that survives from the period before 750, and that is if one includes the early copy of Adómnan's *Life of Columba* which seems to have been taken to the continent from Iona shortly after its creation.[8] That makes it hard to know exactly how Adómnan's work fitted within hagiographical production in Britain and Ireland in the seventh century. The earliest witness to the texts about St. Patrick, the famous Book of Armagh, is ninth-century, while the earliest witness to the two oldest (seventh-century) lives of Brigit is tenth-century and continental.[9] There are only two unpalimpsested Merovingian hagiographical manuscripts that are certainly from before 750, and none from the English kingdoms or Spain, so the texts we use rest on identifications and reconstructions based on later materials there, too. Our knowledge of Greek and Syrian hagiography often rests on no firmer foundations.[10] Philology and the tracing of "archaic" linguistic features can be useful, but you cannot please all academics all of the time, and people will always argue on the basis of "feeling," even against the most imperious of Latinists. We need not go into the technicalities involved in these debates—it is better to enjoy them first-hand and I am not an imperious Latinist anyway—but the underlying problems raise some issues of interest to our wider project.

First of all, why are there so few early manuscripts? There are two answers, one interesting and one rather banal. The banal answer is simply that we do not know, but there are plenty of fires, wars, and library culls in history—perhaps many, as old-fashioned texts have been updated, replaced, or copied more legibly—which clearly have not been kind to the overall survival rate of manuscripts. The more interesting answer is "technological change." Certainly in the late Roman world, through to the time of Gregory of Tours, many hagiographies circulated written on papyrus rolls. In his *Life of the Fathers*, Gregory mentions a miracle concerning one on

Nicetius of Lyon (bk. 8, chap. 12). But papyrus is not very robust and does not survive well in the damper climates north of the Mediterranean. One can compare this situation to the difficulties of reconstructing early Hindu traditions in regions that used fragile palm-leaf manuscripts, with virtually none left extant from before the ninth century.[11] Our knowledge of Merovingian bureaucratic culture rests almost exclusively on the chance survival of a number of papyrus legal documents from St. Denis in France, themselves dreadfully fragile and in a poor state; yet presumably if St. Denis had such documents, many religious institutions and even private secular individuals had them, and that probably means hundreds of thousands of documents have been lost. Later copies of Merovingian legal formularies would suggest so. How different the so-called "Dark Ages" could look to us! For Gaul, the big technological shift was the move to using parchment (dried and treated animal skins), which survived much better. The problems of papyrus durability may explain the poor survival rate of early Italian texts from before the seventh century. Other regions, including Ireland and Germany, presumably never had this exact transition to make in the same way, but we do not know what we might have lost from writings on slate or bark.

The manuscripts we do have show a variety of organizational principles. (Big digitization projects such as e-codices in Switzerland make it easy for anyone to examine these and you are encouraged to have a look.) Some manuscripts contained just one, maybe two, texts, if those texts were on the long side.[12] The scribe Dorbbene who copied the earliest witness of the *Life of Columba* added no other full text to his creation, perhaps because of its length (136 pages), and perhaps because the point of copying it in the first place was to promote Columba and the *Life* (preserved as Schaffhausen, Stiftsbibliothek, Gen. 1). Similar points could be made of other famous monumental Lives in manuscripts, such as the ninth-century Stuttgart copy of Rimbert of Hamburg-Bremen's *Life of Anskar*, a lengthy text designed to encourage support for Rimbert's missionary work in Scandinavia, here possibly targeted at Bishop Solomon of Konstanz.[13] Length was not always decisive. Under Abbot Grimoald, the monastery of Corbie copied the *Life of Wandregisil* in a big, bold uncial script, stretching the modest text to fill sixty-one spacious pages by itself—an almost extravagant use of resources which might say something about Grimoald's effort to foster closer links with the important metropolitan diocese of Rouen.[14] Making a manuscript was time-consuming and expensive. It is not difficult to imagine that the end product was designed for some kind of political end, even if we cannot always prove that.

The act of juxtaposing texts in manuscripts can, by extension, also seem purposeful. It is true that the logic of connections does not always announce itself strongly. There is a manuscript from Verona, neatly executed there in 517, which contains Sulpicius Severus's dossier of texts on St. Martin of Tours, bound with Jerome's *Life of Paul the Hermit* (Verona, Biblioteca Capitolare, MS XXXVIII (36)). The doublet is only thematically coherent in the sense that it concerns figures keen on an ascetic mode of living; if there is more to it than that, particularly with regards to something relevant to sixth-century Verona, it is not obvious. Thematic coherence is, nevertheless, a great leveller. A famous eighth-century manuscript from Eichstätt brings together Willibald's *Life of Boniface* with the multi-layered doublet the *Life of Wynnebald and Willibald*, work which extends the story of Boniface's work in Bavaria but which also has embedded in it Willibald's own account of his pilgrimage to the Holy Land.[15] In terms of hagiographical commonplaces, the account of Willibald is deeply unsettling because he wrote or dictated significant portions, does not seem to have been dead when Hugeberc produced the final draft, and the emphasis on sanctity is squarely on his brother Wynnebald, whose incorrupt body Willibald had reburied in a lavish ceremony.[16] In this case, what made the story of Willibald part of a hagiographical canon was its textual and manuscript relationship to compositions that look more squarely like sacred biographies.

An important development in the archiving of hagiography was the production of legendaries—grand compilations of *acta, passiones*, and *vitae*.[17] The earliest of these are comprised significantly of the *gesta martyrum* of pre-Constantinian male and female saints, with texts composed between the fifth and the seventh centuries.[18] In his letter, as we saw, Pope Gregory the Great mentioned only being able to find one such collection in the papal archive or Roman libraries, although this by no means should be read as saying that other centres lacked them or that Rome was short of individual texts (maybe also written on fragile papyrus). Efforts such as Defourcq's *Étude sur les Gesta martyrum romains* (5 vols., 1886–1910) to identify in extant manuscripts any core Roman collection which may have resembled that in Gregory's single manuscript have not met with success.[19] The extant compilations may share many texts, but there is no stable core in content or order for the Roman material. Moreover, most of the compilations are demonstrably post-750 products from north of the Alps and demonstrate plenty of exchange between the Roman, Frankish, Spanish, and Lombard worlds over a long period of time. We can take the texts individually, but at the level of the legendaries themselves we find that we are locked into a hagiographical thought-world that stretches later and further north than late-antique Rome.

It is worth taking time to consider the variety that one of these early legendaries contains. For the sake of illustration, I will take the example of Paris, Bibliothèque nationale de France, MS lat. 12598, written in two northern centres, one possibly Maastricht, in the late eighth or early ninth century, and later housed in the library of Corbie.[20] It is not necessarily the easiest manuscript to analyze, as it is made up of at least three thematic units (1–3, 4, and 5–7), and the first half of 4 seems to have been an incomplete copy of a text from one centre finished off at another. These are the contents:

1. **Martinellum (ff. 1–22).** The legendary starts with the dossier of material on St. Martin compiled by Sulpicius Severus and with an extra story from Gregory of Tours' *Histories* (bk. 2, chap. 1). Together, the texts relate how

the soldier-saint from Illyricum found his vocation and lived as both ascetic and bishop in Tours, with accounts of posthumous miracles to prove his power.

2. **Merovingian-Era Gallic Confessor-Saints (ff. 23–32):** Remigius of Reims (d. 533), Medardus of Noyon (d. ca. 545), and Vedastus of Arras (d. ca. 540). The *Life of Remigius* is a late reworking of a lost Merovingian text, the *Life of Medardus* was addressed to King Theudebert II (r. 596–612), and the *Life of Vedastus* was composed by Jonas of Bobbio in the seventh century.[21] Remigius and Vedastus were both said to have been involved in the conversion of King Clovis (d. 511), the first convert Frankish king. Medardus benefited from the patronage of Clovis's son Chlotar I.
3. **Earlier Martyrs from Gaul (ff. 32–46).** It starts with the story of the martyrdom of Fuscianus, Victoricus, and Gentianus of Amiens, which is part of the "Rictiovarus Cycle" of martyrdom stories set in the third century but composed in the seventh. This is complemented by the stories of Justus of Auxerre and Lucianus, both martyred in Beauvais. Next, there is the story of Crispin and Crispinian, the martyred shoemakers of Soissons. The section concludes with the first part of the Latin translation of the apocryphal *Martyrium Matthaei*, about the death of Matthew the Apostle; it breaks off, however, at the end of the first full page, as the rest of that part of the manuscript has been lost.
4. **Two Northern Saints (ff. 47–61).** This section starts with Servatius of Tongeren, a fourth-century church-builder who was prominent in the orthodox fight against Arianism. Geography provides the common factor as the account of Servatius is followed by the eighth-century story of Lambert of Maastricht (d. 705), the

controversial bishop who spent a decade in political exile and who was "martyred" in the course of a dispute (see Chapter 1). The choice of saints was not initially made at the same scribal centre as the rest of the manuscript, as the whole of the *Life of Servatius* and the first half of the *Life of Lambert* form a discrete codicological unit and are written in a different script, possibly in Maastricht (ff. 47–53). Nevertheless, the *Life of Lambert* was then finished off at the first centre, so we get to witness a different way that people brought texts together in manuscripts here.

5. **Female Virgin Martyrs (ff. 62–105):** Cecilia of Rome, who convinced her husband to preserve her purity with the help of an angel, but who was later beheaded for her beliefs; Euphemia of Chalcedon, who was publicly tortured to death after refusing to make sacrifices to the gods; Agnes of Rome, who as an avowed Christian was stripped and threatened with rape before being impaled by a sword; Agatha of Catania, who rejected the advances of a prefect and was imprisoned, first in a brothel and then in a prison, where she was tortured until she died; and finally Lucia of Syracuse, who, inspired by Agatha, narrowly avoided having her purity defiled in another brothel and survived efforts to burn her alive before she was killed by the sword, all for refusing to make a sacrifice to pagan gods. A sixth text, on Columba of Sens, is similar in that the heroine is imprisoned in a brothel for refusing marriage and narrowly avoids being burned to death before being killed by a sword; only the settings of the story differ, as she comes from Spain, suffers in Vienne, and is buried in the north of Gaul in Sens.

6. **Constantius's Life of Germanus of Auxerre (ff. 105–7),** about the fifth-century bishop who fought heresy in Britain. It seems out of place in the run of virgin

martyrs. Perhaps the scriptorium meant to include it earlier in the manuscript but something went wrong.

7. **Another Virgin Martyr (ff. 107–9),** Juliana of Nicomedia, who was tortured and beheaded for refusing marriage—a story which clearly fits well with section 5, and highlighting further the oddity of the placing of Germanus's story.

The compilation as a whole raises important issues about the relationships between different types of saint. They are broadly grouped as male confessors, then male martyrs, then female martyrs. At the same time, the manner of compilation, with no subheadings, brings the saints to the same level regardless of gender, manner of death, or the time or place in which they lived. They all represent the single "life of the saint" which Gregory of Tours talked about. In the process, many of the things we think are important about saints' Lives are collapsed, such as the authorial agenda behind them or their reflections of contemporary social dynamics. A monk in Corbie at the turn of the ninth century would have read from the legendary about Remigius of Reims, Lambert of Maastricht, and Agnes of Rome for their spiritual lessons, rather than for their situational textual arguments. The texts contextualize each other and add new emphases to the holy life through common themes and motifs.

The power of texts to function collectively as well as individually helped to define the stature of new saints and new compositions about them. Willibald's *Life of Boniface* quickly found a new home in a northern French manuscript in which Boniface's new sanctity was placed alongside established figures including Ambrose, Jerome, Martin, and Benedict—effectively communicating that there was little difference between old and new sanctity.[22] An early scribe in St. Gallen saw no problem making a *Suffering of St Leudegar of Autun* the only relatively modern and northern text in a collection of martyrs' tales, presumably again because martyrs belonged together regardless of their historical circumstances.[23]

Carolingian compilers of legendaries also added Merovingian texts on Queen Radegund (in the Turin Legendary) and Abbess Gertrude of Nivelles (in the Montpellier Legendary) to runs of texts on virgin saints in early legendaries. Such juxtapositions defined newer saints and texts by projecting a sense of shared authenticity with the old. The promotion of newer saints was probably never a principal purpose of legendaries that mixed in newer material; nevertheless, the point was that all saints belonged together.

To achieve their aims, sometimes compilers of texts needed to tailor their source material. A crude example of this is the textual history of Gregory the Great's *Life of Benedict*, which began life as book two of four in the *Dialogues*, but which soon circulated as a coherent text in its own right, as we have seen with the *vita patrum* manuscript that included the *Life of Boniface*. The story of Benedict was too appealing to audiences across the West to remain shackled to Gregory's parade of more obscure Italian saints and reflections on judgement. More common was the abbreviation of texts, as we find with ninth-century versions of the Merovingian *Life of Amandus of Maastricht* and the continental reductions of the Irish *Life of Columba of Iona* (which tended to miss out the unusual Irish names).[24] We have also encountered, in Chapter 1, the importance of rewriting texts to meet both new literary and new political demands, and that practice of *réécriture* (rewriting) undoubtedly played out in relation to concerns about copying and collecting texts more generally.

Some of these collections of texts reflect cultic activities and liturgical cycles better than others. One manuscript from Salzburg ca. 800 is clearly arranged so that the sequence of texts follows the sequence of saints' feasts on a calendar, which suggests one context for use: to provide stories for use in church services.[25] One from Corbie from around the same time, now known as the "Turin Legendary," seems less systematic. A major compilation from St. Gallen includes, rather than a contents list, a calendar which indicates when a text might be relevant and whether it was in the large, small, or new passionary ("so that you, reader, may more easily find them," noted one later scribe in an introduction), but the contents themselves are not arranged in calendrical order.[26] This might suggest that the compilation was intended for study and meditation as well as to provide material for preaching. Since no two legendaries are the same, it is essential to treat each on their own terms, to see what organization says about intended use. At same time, we should probably not imagine that people were bound by the intentions of the original scribes—particularly generations later, if the books were still used.

Once we are dealing with substantial compilations and indeed whole libraries, one needs to ask to what extent these collected texts represented local "cults of saints." Was possession of a text the same as studied devotion towards a saint? One suspects not. Many shrines attracted people without anyone necessarily having a text of any sort (see the belated effort to write a *Life of Sualo* mentioned in Chapter 1), while there were plenty of texts which connected the reader to distant people and places with which they would have had no other association (as with Charles the Bald and St. Demetrios). Hagiographies and local cults were not dependent on each other. The circulation of historiographical hagiographies shows that interest in them, for edificatory, intellectual, and literary reasons, often far exceeded the initial intended use and audience. The implications of this observation is important. Where, as we shall see in Chapter 3, modern scholars have seen hagiography written as "cult propaganda" and "ecclesiastical swindle literature," much of it has survived through a less discerning effort to collect stories about the holy in all their forms.

Calendars, Martyrologies, Litanies

Gregory the Great, in his letter to Eulogius of Alexandria, mentioned that he suspected his colleague already had an alternative to a collection of hagiographical narratives: a single volume which listed the martyrs and their place of death but with no other historical information. Gregory was describing what we would normally call a "martyrology." It may technically be possible to maintain a distinction between such a text and a calendar which listed feasts, maybe on the basis of whether it was part of a liturgical text or a "computus"; often, however, the distinction was of little practical importance. By the eighth century, in England and on the continent, priests were encouraged in penitentials and legislation to possess a martyrology (and a separate computus) as part of their standard "weapons" (*arma*) for preaching. There was demand for expanded versions of the martyrologies as hagiographical digests which reduced the need to carry around multiple volumes. Other bits of useful information could be added, too, making some such as the *Old English Martyrology* into veritable encyclopaedias.[27] These all provide essential context for understanding the organizational structures of hagiography and cult.

One of the oldest surviving calendars listing saints' feasts belonged to someone himself later celebrated as a saint: St. Willibrord (d. 739).[28] Willibrord's long career took him far: he grew up in his native Northumbria, trained for a while as a monk in southern Ireland, and became a missionary in Frisia in 690, bishop of Utrecht in 695, and abbot of Echternach (in what is now Luxembourg) a few years later, with political connections stretching to the Main Valley. The calendar reflects these journeys, with names from across the regions in which he lived. This included memorial notices for the deaths of Northumbrian kings Ecgfrith and Oswald, Irish saints Patrick and Brigit, and Frankish saints Sulpicius of Bourges and Amandus of Maastricht. These are set within a tapestry of entries for feasts such as Christmas, patristic saints including Ambrose of Milan and Jerome, old martyrs such as Perpetua and Felicity or Valentine, and the apostles. A number of personal memorial notes rest alongside these saints, including two in red to "Suidberht the priest" (a character mentioned by Bede) and "Oethiluald the monk" (about whom we know nothing). The calendar provided a space in which the names of the cherished dead from across time and space could come together to be remembered—not just by

Willibrord, but by the whole community who partook in the creation and use of the document.

Calendars are one of the many kinds of source which are not "historiographical hagiographies" but which worked alongside such texts. We have already seen one example of a calendar being used in St. Gallen to help coordinate the use of hagiography. While that example is unusual, the transmission and circulation of calendars was an important part of how people came to hear about saints. Litanies, in which saints were listed to be invoked during the liturgy, also contributed to the promotion of names.[29] Neither was necessarily tied to dedicated cults of saints, as perhaps exposed by the surprise presence of St. Medardus of Soissons in English litanies, or the ninth-century calendar from Hildesheim that lists two feasts for the English martyrs Hewald the White and Hewald the Black simply because the scribe had found different spellings of their names and assumed them to be two different saint pairs.[30] Such oddities again expose just how often hagiographical discourse was less about connecting with a verifiable sacred history, and more about engaging with a more abstract spiritual world in which it was more important that something was powerful than whether anyone knew what it was.

Martyrologies were an important resource here, straddling the worlds of historical narration and lists of saints.[31] The most famous early martyrology is probably that associated with Jerome but probably composed later in the fifth century and indeed only available to us now in edited versions from the seventh century onwards. Coincidentally, the oldest manuscript is bound to Willibrord's calendar and was copied under him by the Echternach scribe Laurentius. The text Laurentius had was a bare list of martyrs for each day of the calendar year, with saints from East and West, updated with a couple of names associated with the circle of St. Columbanus in Burgundy and Lombardy. In listing saints for every day of the year, it went far beyond the project of a calendar such as Willibrord's, which exhibits a more selective approach to veneration and memorial activities. Moreover, it added a spatial dimension to commemorating saints by listing to where a saint belonged ("21st January, Rome, the holy virgin Agnes"), just as Gregory the Great had outlined. From such bare bones, a tradition of compiling encyclopaedias of sanctity developed.

The earliest full historical martyrology is associated with Bede in early eighth-century Northumbria.[32] Bede built on the foundations of the Hieronymian martyrology—or at least a version of it—but he created something more elaborate, rather like a hagiographical digest summarizing the sufferings of the martyrs from their *gesta*. Staying with the example of St. Agnes, he elaborated that "under the prefect of the city Symphronius, having been tossed into the fires, but those fires having been extinguished through her prayers, [Agnes] was pierced through by the sword." It is clear from this and a great many other entries that Bede had access to a broad selection of the *gesta martyrum* and *vitae patrum*, partly thanks to his abbots' efforts to acquire resources from Rome for Wearmouth–Jarrow, and no doubt also from other ad hoc acquisitions from around Europe. (In the south at the same time, Aldhelm of Malmesbury had access to the same kinds of works for his *On Virginity* which we encountered in Chapter 1.) There is a striking paucity of figures from Ireland, the English kingdoms, and Gaul, but this may simply reflect his interest in creating access to authentic old stories about bodily suffering, for which the confessors who dominated northern tradition were less interesting.[33] Continental writers, editing and expanding Bede's work over the next century, took a different stance and added many stories about non-martyrs for the edification of their readers anyway.

The exact use of these extended martyrologies is not clear and may not have been uniform. The evidence of Gregory and the early Hieronymian Martyrology points to liturgical use: the reading out of names as part of Mass. This connects to that instruction to priests, popularized across the West from an eighth-century penitential, that they should each have a martyrology as part of their standard armoury. Yet, as John McCulloh argued in a 1983 study of historical martyrologies, there were intellectual endeavours here, too.[34] Both Hrabanus Maurus and Usuard alluded to the problems people faced in finding information about saints and their feast days spread across a variety of books, sometimes with contradictory information. Notker the Stammerer of St. Gallen, right at the end of the ninth century, explicitly addressed issues with several of his stories where he had found problems with his source material. The act of compiling a single dossier on the saints had an edificatory purpose, but that purpose meant responsibilities towards accuracy.

There was some niggling doubt about the authenticity of some collections of stories. The most controversial was probably that produced by Ado of Vienne, at least to judge by the defensive preface to the second version of the work.[35] "You should not think of me working in an empty space" he began—an opening gambit which immediately sounds suspicious. For a start, he claimed, he only added saints to days which did not have any in his teacher Florus of Lyon's martyrology, which itself built on the work of "Lord Bede." Not only that, but he pointed out that he had access to a "venerable and very old martyrology from the city of Rome, sent to a certain holy bishop of Aquileia by the Roman pontiff, and later passed on to me by a certain religious brother of some days." Naturally, he transcribed the "venerable and very old martyrology from Rome" to prove his case, although it is not entirely clear why, if it is what he claimed, it contained an entry for the seventh-century hermit St. Goar (d. 649) who died in Oberwesel, or Pope Martin (d. 655), or indeed one for St. Patrick. It also seems to contain the earliest confusion of Boniface of Mainz and his namesake Bonifatius of Tarsus, as it gives the English martyr's feast day (June 5) as the date of the Roman martyr's burial. It was all probably an attempt, anyway, to create authority for his implausible claim that Crescentius, first bishop of Vienne, was the disciple of Paul.

Metrical or poetic martyrologies point towards the value of the texts for study. The oldest of these is by Oengus of Tallaght, who wrote in Old Irish early in the ninth century. Oengus gives no specific reason for either the decision to write poetry or to eschew Latin; his text is otherwise a relatively standard Hieronymian-style martyrology with more Irish entries, prefaced by a celebration of the eternal power of Christ and his saints in contrast to the transitory nature of earthly power. The second-oldest was composed only a decade later in ca. 848 in Prüm by the monk Wandalbert, with help from his friend Florus of Lyon. The tally of two texts may not be impressive—more would come in the tenth century—but, alongside the proliferation of narrative martyrologies in the ninth century, it is a testament to the energy and creativity involved in understanding the whole cult of saints in the period.

As Gregory suggested, Western traditions had their Eastern counterparts. These can broadly be divided into synaxaria, which provided hagiographical notes as part of liturgical handbooks, and menologia, which contained full hagiographical texts in order of their feast days. The two most famous are both from the tenth century: the *Synaxarion of Constantinople* and the multivolume *Metaphrastic Menologion* of Simeon Metaphrastes.[36] But, as Claudia Rapp has stressed, these represented a particular pair of organizational high points that emerged from a rich but mostly lost history.[37] Exactly how one gets from Gregory and Eulogius to a world in which legendaries and martyrologies were common remains unclear. The similarities of developments over the intervening centuries, given the different histories otherwise, raises intriguing issues about structural similarities in the organization of hagiography and cult.

Conclusion: Changing Practices

We set out in this chapter to examine the ways in which stories about saints were organized and circulated. The point of this, as I hope is clear by now, is that it is not always enough simply to read "the classic biography" if one wants to find out about a saint or a text written about them. Texts were not stable; their precise meaning varied according to the company they kept, they were supplemented by cults and calendars, and more than anything they belonged naturally to wider bodies of stories about saints. Sometimes a hagiographer might have written a text with all this in mind, but more often texts enjoyed an afterlife all of their own, dependent entirely on what other people in other contexts wanted with them. At the same time, however, this all shows that habits of thinking about hagiography seemed to change. Eulogius's query about a compendium of saints' deeds seemed odd to Gregory the Great in 598 because he could only think of one big collection; by the late ninth century, it looks as if such things could be found far and wide, in some form or other. While we might find that many aspects of hagiographical texts stayed the same, it is clear that we must always be attentive to the changing practices that surrounded those texts if we want to understand anything about the pasts of which they were part.

Notes

[1] Thomas Heffernan, *Sacred Biography: Saints and their Biographers in the Middle Ages* (Oxford: Oxford University Press, 1988).

[2] These texts can be found in *Vitae sanctorum Hiberniae*, ed. Heist, 160–67 and 182–98.

[3] Susan Ashbrook Harvey, *Asceticism and Society in Crisis: John of Ephesus and the Lives of the Eastern Saints* (Berkeley: University of California Press, 1990).

[4] John Kieschnick, *The Eminent Monk: Buddhist Ideals in Medieval Chinese Hagiography* (Honolulu: University of Hawai'i Press, 1997).

[5] On these texts see Raymond Van Dam, *Saints and their Miracles in Late Antique Gaul* (Berkeley: University of California Press, 1991).

[6] Richard Shaw, "Chronology, Composition, and Authorial Conception in the *Miracula*," in *A Companion to Gregory of Tours*, ed. Alexander Callander Murray (Leiden: Brill, 2016), 102–40.

[7] *Paul the Deacon: Liber de episcopis Mettensibus*, ed. and trans. Damien Kempf (Leuven: Peeters, 2013).

[8] Schaffhausen, Stadtbibliothek, MS Gen. 1, online at www.e-codices.unifr.ch/en/list/one/sbs/0001. See also now *The*

Schaffhausen Adomnán, ed. Damien Bracken and Eric Graff (Cork: Cork University Press, 2014).

[9] The Book of Armagh is in Dublin, Trinity College Library, MS 52; online at www.confessio.ie/manuscripts/dublin#1.

[10] Claudia Rapp, "Figures of Female Sanctity: Byzantine Edifying Manuscripts and their Audience," *Dumbarton Oaks Papers* 50 (1996): 313–44.

[11] One of the oldest dates from only the ninth century: a copy of the Pārameśvaratantra, online at http://cudl.lib.cam.ac.uk/view/MS-ADD-01049-00001/9.

[12] For a survey of such early surviving manuscripts, see Joseph-Claude Poulin, "Les *Libelli* dans l'edition hagiographique avant le XIIe siècle," in *Livrets, Collections et Textes. Études sur la tradition hagiographique latin*, ed. Martin Heinzelmann (Ostfildern: Thorbecke, 2006), 15–194.

[13] Stuttgart, Württembergische Landesbibliothek, MS HB XIV 7: http://digital.wlb-stuttgart.de/sammlungen/sammlungsliste/werksansicht/?no_cache=1&tx_dlf[id]=4176&tx_dlf[page]=1&cHash=34f59bcd6c05dceb5e01e73a1db1c7d5.

[14] Paris, Bibliothèque nationale de France, MS lat. 18315: http://gallica.bnf.fr/ark:/12148/btv1b85935666.r=latin%2018315?rk=21459;2.

[15] Munich, Bayerische Landesbibliothek, Clm. 1086: http://daten.digitale-sammlungen.de/~db/0006/bsb00064004/images/.

[16] James T. Palmer, *Anglo-Saxons in a Frankish World, 690–900* (Turnhout: Brepols, 2009), 249–69.

[17] Guy Philippart, *Les légendiers latins et autres manuscrits hagiographiques* (Turnhout: Brepols, 1977).

[18] On many of these, see now Michael Lapidge, *The Roman Martyrs* (Oxford: Oxford University Press, 2018).

[19] Clare Pilsworth, "Dating the *Gesta martyrum*: A Manuscript-Based Approach," *Early Medieval Europe* 9 (2000): 309–24.

[20] *CLA* 644a and 644b. A microfilm is available online here: http://gallica.bnf.fr/ark:/12148/btv1b9066719b.r=latin%2012598?rk=21459;2. David Ganz, *Corbie in the Carolingian Renaissance* (Sigmaringen: Thorbecke, 1991), 129.

[21] For these and other references to Merovingian texts, see Martin Heinzelmann, "L'hagiographie mérovingienne. Panorama des documents potentiels," in *L'hagiographie mérovingienne à travers ses réécritures*, ed. Martin Heinzelmann, Monique Goullet, and Christiane Veyrard-Cosme (Ostfildern: Thorbecke, 2010), 27–82.

[22] St. Gallen, Stiftsbibliothek, MS 552: www.e-codices.unifr.ch/en/searchresult/list/one/csg/0552. *CLA* 942.

[23] St. Gallen, Stiftsbibliothek, MS 563: www.e-codices.unifr.ch/en/searchresult/list/one/csg/0563.

[24] *Vita Amandi* is abbreviated in Würzburg, Universitätsbibliothek, MS Mp.th.q.15. The *Vita Columba* is partially abbreviated in St. Gallen, Stiftsbibliothek, MS 555, with more substantial reductions in Munich, Bayerische Staatsbibliothek, Clm 6341 and London, British Library, MS Add. 19726.

[25] Max Diesenberger, "Der CVP 420—die Gemeinschaft der Heiligen und ihre Gestaltung im frühmittelalterlichen Bayern," in *L'Hagiographie mérovingienne*, 219–48.

[26] St. Gallen, Stiftsbibliothek, MS 566, with the note on p. 1: www.e-codices.unifr.ch/en/searchresult/list/one/csg/0566. The foundational study of this manuscript is Emmauel Munding, *Das Verzeichnis der St Galler Heiligenleben und ihrer Handschriften in Codex Sangall. No. 566* (Leipzig: Harrassowitz, 1918).

[27] Christine Rauer, *The Old English Martyrology* (Cambridge: Brewer, 2013).

[28] *The Calendar of Willibrord*, ed. H. A. Wilson (London: Henry Bradshaw Society, 1918). The original is Paris, Bibliothèque nationale, lat. 10837: http://gallica.bnf.fr/ark:/12148/btv1b6001113z/f2.item. On early calendars see Arno Borst, *Die karolingische Kalenderreform* (Hanover: Hahn, 1998).

[29] Michael Lapidge, *Anglo-Saxon Litanies of the Saints* (London: Henry Bradshaw Society, 1991).

[30] Bernhard Bischoff, "Das karolingische Kalendar der Palimpsesthandschrift Ambros. M. 12 sup," in *Colligere fragmenta*, ed. Bonifatius Fischer and Virgil Fiala (Beuron: Erzabtei Beuron, 1952), 247–60.

[31] Henri Quentin, *Les martyrologes historiques du moyen âge—étude sur la formation du martyrologe romain* (Paris: Gabalda, 1908).

[32] Alan Thacker, "Bede and his Martyrology," in *Listen, O Isles, Unto Me: Studies in Medieval Word and Image in Honour of Jennifer O'Reilly*, ed. Elizabeth Mullins and Diarmuid Scully (Cork: Cork University Press, 2010), 126–41.

[33] John M. McCulloh, "Historical Martyrologies in the Benedictine Cultural Tradition," in *Benedictine Culture 750–1050*, ed. W. Lourdaux and D. Verhelst (Leuven: Leuven University Press, 1983), 114–31.

[34] John M. McCulloh, "Historical Martyrologies", 114–31.

[35] *Le martyrologe d'Adon: ses deux familles, ses trois recensions*, ed. Jacques Dubois (Paris: Éditions du Centre National de la Recherche Scientifique, 1984).

[36] Andrea Luzzi, "Synaxaria and the Synaxarion of Constantinople," *Ashgate Research Companion to Byzantine Hagiography* 2, ed. Stephanos Efthymiadis (Farnham: Ashgate, 2014), 197–298; Christian Høgel, "Symeon Metaphrastes and the Metaphrastic Movement," *Ashgate Research Companion to Byzantine Hagiography* 2, 181–96; and Claudia Rapp, "Byzantine Hagiographers as Antiquarians, Seventh to Ninth Centuries," *Byzantinische Forschung* 21 (1995): 31–44 at 31–33.

[37] Rapp, "Byzantine Hagiographers," and her "Figures of Female Sanctity."

Chapter 3

Historians and the Quest for Truth

What are the motives and methodologies for modern historians writing about saints? If Chapters 1 and 2 demonstrated that the saintly past was rarely packaged value-free for posterity, the purpose of the present chapter is to sketch some of the ways that this is no less true of modern scholarship on hagiography. Religious beliefs, theoretical dispositions, and stylistic sensibilities each affect the perceived value of saints' stories as historical sources. These bring with them different attitudes to what might constitute appropriate—maybe even "scientific"—methods for analyzing medieval texts. It remains easy for historians to claim that, if we "read with care"—i.e., check for biases and dismiss anything that sounds implausible like the miraculous—then we are left with straightforward accounts of a historical past. But we need to be cannier than that. Bias is essential to understanding polemic and mentality. "Implausible" episodes are still integral parts of the story. Modern historians are (inevitably) capable of imposing their own agendas and dispositions onto the past, even when they have the best intentions. We need better-defined analytical tools than just raw common sense and aesthetic judgements. In what follows, we will encounter some of the heroes and anti-heroes who have attempted to develop different approaches to hagiography, and the paradigms they have helped to create. I don't advocate any particular approach: indeed, I hope the reader will find inspiration and useful questions throughout that might be redeployed and recombined to help generate new studies.

The present chapter is also supposed to work in tandem with Chapter 4. There, readers will find discussion of the ways in which modern studies of hagiography have changed how we view crucial aspects of the early Middle Ages. One can have all the tools in the world, but one has to see them in action sometimes to know what difference they actually make—although, hopefully, this will also be clear in what follows. Together, the two chapters address an important issue that haunts studies of the past in all its forms: the way you study it will affect the way that it seems, regardless of what happened.

Great Enterprises and Beyond: The Bollandists and Monumenta Germaniae Historica

The modern study of hagiography goes back, in spirit, to the work of the Bollandists. This began in earnest in 1630 when Jean Bolland started to develop the project of Heribert Rosweyde (d. 1629) to publish saints' Lives taken from manuscripts.[1] The scholars involved intended their work to be a response to scholarship in the Reformation in which Lives were abbreviated or had elements suppressed to fit new sensibilities. In some of those oldest volumes produced for the resulting *Acta Sanctorum* series, it is no longer always clear precisely what the source manuscripts were, as some did not yet have library shelfmarks, and many failed to survive the following centuries. The level of methodological rigour began to change under the influence of Charles de Smedt (d. 1911), who wanted texts edited with the kind of critical precision being developed elsewhere in Europe for non-hagiographical works—that is, with consideration of textual variants and families, alongside some level of historical commentary. This led to the launch of the journal *Analecta Bollandiana* in 1882, which often included transcriptions of hagiographical texts from specific individual manuscripts (starting with St. Boniface of Mainz).[2] In 1898 the first volume of the *Bibliotheca Hagiographica Latina* was published, which assigned a number to every hagiographical text (so the *Life of Boniface* was *BHL* 1400, the *Second Life of Boniface* was *BHL* 1401, and so on). This complemented the *Bibliotheca Hagiographica Graeca*, launched in 1895, and the *Bibliotheca Hagiographica Orientalis*, which was first published in 1910. The assignment of *BHL*, *BHG*, and *BHO* numbers helped to disambiguate discussions of stories about saints while identifying what Lives for each saint there were for study.

One of the leading lights of the Bollandists' "Golden Age" (as they call it on their website) was Hippolyte Delehaye (d. 1941). In 1927, late in his career, Delehaye declared that he hoped that his work would do for hagiography what Jean Mabillon (d. 1707) had done for diplomatics—namely, establish sufficiently rigorous criteria for separating the authentic from the forged. That comment came in the preface to the third edition of his famous handbook, *Les légends hagiographiques*, first published in 1905 and first translated into English in 1907 as *Legends of the Saints*. It provided a blistering critique of how many people in Delehaye's own time interpreted saints' Lives, particularly those in the Church rather than professional historians as such. He raised many important issues, some of which may seem obvious, but which needed saying and often still do. These included paying attention to the hagiographer's own context and agenda, the impositions of literary forms on stories, the problems posed by authors using both written and oral source material, and the compulsion of everyone involved, medieval and modern, to fill in gaps in knowledge with educated guesswork. He concluded by pointing out a number of common errors in using saints' Lives: not separating a historical saint from his or her legend, excessive trust in hagiographers, incautious appeal to local tradition to disprove scholarly conclusions, and declaring that a narrative is true simply because it seems probable or accurate in some regards (i.e., the "reading with care" fallacy) without proper investigation. These were all good warnings a century ago, and they remain useful to anyone reading saints' stories now.

Where does Delehaye's critique lead us? The man himself believed that it provided a firmer basis for establishing the historicity of many saints. Scientific rigour reinforced truth all the more for having exposed where falsehood lay, even if it often led to a heightened understanding of literary form rather than the past it described. Many subsequent critics appreciated this intention in Delehaye's work if nothing else. After postmodernists challenged received ideas of historical truth by highlighting the gap between language and reality, the American historian Patrick Geary was perfectly justified in sarcastically proclaiming the following:[3]

> We should not pretend that Jacques Derrida has revealed something radically new to us: that hagiography reproduces hagiography rather than some putative reality. Hippolyte Delehaye pointed this out in 1905 in his *Legends of the Saints*, although because he wrote in plain, comprehensible language, his message was perhaps not as clear as that of Derrida.

This is not to say that Delehaye had somehow pre-empted postmodernism, of course, but rather to identify him as the champion of a solid, rigorous approach to sifting through hagiographical narratives as literature without resorting to jargon. Dealing with the literary character of hagiographies may seem inconvenient to many researchers and readers, but it has a long history and it is unavoidable. It does not, of course, mean the stories aren't based on historical events. It also does not mean that legendary saints weren't an integral part of the cultural make-up of many communities, Eastern and Western.

The common sense of separating truth and fiction still meant different things to different people. Charles Plummer (d. 1927), an interested contemporary of Delehaye's who himself edited English and Irish hagiography, found it necessary to comment "unfavourably" on Bede's accounts of the miraculous: "Many may be condemned summarily on internal evidence, being silly, unspiritual, or even positively immoral," he argued in his 1896 edition of Bede's historical works (*Venerabilis Baedae Opera Historicae*, p. lxiv). Here wrote the chaplain of Corpus Christi College, Oxford, note, not a fierce atheist. At least Plummer kept the texts he edited intact, even if his editorial method was at times somewhat enigmatic.[4] Some scholars, no more impressed than Plummer, sometimes felt that the inclusion of doubtful material was not always necessary for the presentation of historical documents in modern editions. And this is where we come to work of the Monumenta Germaniae Historica (MGH).

In many respects, the work of Bruno Krusch (d. 1940) for the MGH represented the kind of scientific rigour that de Smedt and Delehaye had imagined for studies of hagiography.[5] The organization was dedicated to establishing trustworthy editions of all texts pertaining to early Germanic history, interpreted broadly so as to include many late-antique and early-medieval texts from across Europe. To achieve this for the Merovingian period, Krusch's MGH sub-series *Scriptores rerum Merovingicarum* produced seven volumes between 1885 and 1920, packed mostly with hagiographical material, with the hagiography arranged in chronological order by saint regardless of when the texts themselves were produced. A wealth of manuscript evidence was acquired and processed to help establish original texts, as methodically as possible, with full disclosure of manuscript details and textual variants and families. During this time, major volumes were also produced on Carolingian-era saints for the *Scriptores in folio* sub-series by Oswald Holder-Egger and Georg Waitz as a supplement to the chronicles edited earlier in the century; Krusch produced a further volume dedicated to Venantius Fortunatus in the sub-series *Auctores antiquissimi* and a number of longer Lives—notably Rimbert's *Life of Anskar* and Willibald's *Life of Boniface*—appeared in the sub-series *Scriptores rerum Germanicarum in usum scholarum separatim editi*. Such volumes still provide much of the raw material for studying the early Middle Ages today.

Krusch, it has to be said, was not impressed by much of what he edited. He famously once referred to hagiography as *kirchliche Schwindelliteratur*, "ecclesiastical swindle literature."[6] It was this kind of attitude, shared with many of his colleagues, that led to the omission of miracle stories, theological asides, and accounts of visions—all stories in their view intended to cajole gullible audiences rather than to provide sober history. This led to oddities such as the stripping out of the crucial visionary episodes in the seventh-century *Life of Fursey of Lagny*, despite their absolute centrality to the text. The other problem Krusch had with the material was what he considered the poor state of the Latin and learning more generally. Classical Latinists may sympathize when they encounter some of the grammatical oddities in these early Lives, but some features were undoubtedly reflections of changes in the vernacular away from Classical Latin. Some, however, were the product of Krusch himself accepting some of the textual corruptions in Carolingian and post-Carolingian manuscripts as proof of degenerate learning in Merovingian Gaul, because they confirmed his prejudices.[7] Finally, Krusch's quest to establish the best readings of his texts often led him to present them in forms not quite found in any actual manuscript, notably in the earliest *Suffering of Leudegar* and Jonas's *Life of Columbanus and his Followers*. This is not necessarily a problem—most people are convinced by the reconstructions—but it does mean that many of Krusch's texts as presented are a little artificial. Editorial rigour does not always come value-free.

It was one of Krusch's closest colleagues, Wilhelm Levison, who was one of the first scholars to take the work of the MGH on hagiography and use it to produce nuanced history.[8] His crowning achievement is arguably *England and the Continent in the Eighth Century* (1946), originally delivered in Oxford as the Ford Lectures in 1943 as a conscious effort to help "rejoin broken bonds" between England and Germany during the Second World War, as he noted in the book's preface (see further discussion in Chapter 4). This was political, but it was also personal, as Levison had been forced to flee his homeland for Durham on account of anti-Jewish persecution. Levison had previously edited for MGH the *Lives* of

Willibrord and Boniface, two Englishmen who had worked in Germany, and their stories formed a crucial part of the book. His careful balancing of historiographical narrative against the evidence of letters, histories, and manuscripts was done well, and was all the more potent because he was not fully rooted in the Catholic, Protestant, and/or nationalist polemical traditions that dominated much German historical writing. He urged historians to write about the past on its own terms rather than to impose present debates onto it, leaving contemporary resonance to take care of itself. The careful use of hagiography in post-war accounts of the early Middle Ages was legitimized.

Post-War Moods: From Philology to Sociology

The quest for truth in hagiography took varied directions after the Second World War. Hot on the heels of *England and the Continent*, Cornell-trained Charles W. Jones (d. 1989) produced *Saints' Lives and Chronicles in Early England* (1947), in which he argued that Bede's *vera lex historiae* ("true law of history") was more about finding suitable literary expression for opinions about the past than identifying what actually happened in a strictly factual manner. The truth claims in hagiography and histories do not seem so far apart in this context because they are locked in language. It helped Jones's framing of the issues involved that he was the energetic editor of Bede's scientific works and was well-attuned to issues of form and structure. Issues of literary structure also framed Bertram Colgrave's (d. 1968) 1958 lecture on the historicity of the early Anglo-Saxon saints' Lives, in part pitched as a corrective to Jones's work by the scholar who edited the crucial texts himself between 1927 and his death.[9] For both scholars, the key dynamic at work was the meeting of late-antique hagiographical models—the *Life of Anthony*, Gregory the Great's *Dialogues*, and more—with the heroic tradition that produced the Old English epic *Beowulf*, especially evident in Felix's eighth-century *Life of Guthlac*, in which a former solider hides in marshland, tormented by demons eating snacks. Anglo-Saxon hagiography was well on its way to being used to illustrate Anglo-Saxon society and intellectual life, an enterprise shaped in no small part by the annual Jarrow lectures on the life and times of Bede launched by Colgrave in another 1958 lecture.[10] One just needed sufficient data on the text and context to uncover the logic behind the stories, as we shall see.

Anxiety about models in texts still leads back to thinking about texts as texts, and it always will. For modern philological foundations, one can usefully spend time with Monique Goullet's 2005 study *Écriture et réécriture hagiographiques* ("Writing and Rewriting Hagiographies"). Goullet sought to establish the importance of revisers, editors, and scribes in their own right as authors. Stripping away various textual features to establish an editorial *Urtext* (original text)—say, of a Merovingian original on the basis of a Carolingian copy—is to strip away evidence of reception, intertextuality, scribal practice, and linguistic change which remains an important part of how we should understand hagiography. This is quite different to what Krusch was attempting to do a century earlier. Capturing the necessary evidence effectively is difficult, not least because of the volume of data involved, but digital editions can play an important role here (Goullet, 243–44), enhanced even more now that it is possible to consult so many medieval manuscripts online. In the invaluable Goullet-curated 2014 edition of the Turin Legendary (a collection from Corbie ca. 800), there is a digital appendix of sorts to the printed text which allows one to compare different versions of the same text and digital images of the manuscript. To process all the information from a single collection of just forty texts took a sizeable team of experts to comment on content, language, textual transmission, palaeography, codicology, and liturgical and other contexts. Proceeding in such a manner is labour-intensive. But it is also essential if one wishes to understand more than the simplest and sometimes artificial reconstructions of individual stories.

How do we get from sophisticated understandings of texts to understanding the societies that produced them?

It is František Graus who is often credited with writing the first sustained effort to use hagiography to study society in the early medieval West. Graus was a Communist, trained in Prague, where he was a professor from 1953 until he fled to West Germany during the uncertainties of the Prague Spring of 1969 before eventually settling in Basel. In his work, he was deeply inspired by the work of Marc Bloch and the *Annales* school, which encouraged him to seek methodological inspiration in psychology, sociology, philology, and Marxist theory.[11] In Germany, he was inspired by Helmut Beumann's studies of "mentalities" and the possibility of reconstructing medieval social attitudes on the basis of texts. The first fruit of this approach was *Volk, Herrscher und Heiliger im Reich der Merowinger* ("People, Ruler and Saint in the Kingdom of the Merovingians"), published in 1965, in which Graus used Merovingian hagiography to understand not just social institutions and events, but the ideas around them.[12]

There was little point, in Graus's view, in seeking to establish accurate historical narratives on the basis of saints' Lives as if they were windows onto the past (28–47). Fundamentally, he argued, hagiographical truth was not the same as nineteenth-century ideals of truth, as the former was dedicated to the revealing of spiritual issues, while the latter prioritized issues of causality and sequence with which hagiographers often wilfully dispensed. This was to Graus, echoing Krusch, *Propagandaliteratur* (or "propaganda literature," for anyone easily fazed). The Bollandist project, at least up to Delehaye, was naïve because it sought to extract historical facts on the basis of texts never designed to bear that epistemological weight. It would be like trying to reconstruct the twentieth century on the basis of stylized TV biopics—not impossible, but highly problematic. To ask whether Gregory of Tours' stories of the miraculous were true or not was to ask an inappropriate question. Rather, one should concentrate on understanding the internal logic of the stories as a way of understanding "magic culture" or other ideas of the time. In such suggestions, Graus envisaged using saints' Lives to more anthropological ends, to understand what stories reveal about the values and ideals of a society.

Graus was not alone in starting to think about hagiography as a source for kinds of social history. Friedrich Prinz was pursuing similar ideas in his Munich Habilitation thesis, *Frühes Mönchtum im Frankenreich* ("Early Monasticism in the Frankish Kingdom"), published the same year as *Volk, Herrscher und Heiliger*. An important contribution here was Prinz's sketch of how Merovingian saints' Lives contributed to a "self-construction of noble authority," with the coming together of aristocratic and holy values (14 and 492–93). The theme was developed the same year by his supervisor, Karl Bosl, partly as a swift response to Graus.[13] Meanwhile, in France, Evelyne Patlagean made her own defence of using Byzantine hagiography for social and economic studies in *Annales* in 1968, while preparing *Pauvreté économique et pauvreté sociale à Byzance* (1977) ("Economic Poverty and Social Poverty in Byzantium"). Hagiography was no longer only for religious history.

Before proceeding further, it is worth pausing to reflect on how far we might want to push Graus's ideas. Many historians since 1965 have explicitly or tacitly rejected Graus's notion that truth in hagiographical texts is incompatible with historical truth. We still need, however, a more detailed investigation into early medieval ideals about "historical truth" more generally. In a world of post-truths and alternative facts, we are in little position to take our ideas of truth at face value. The other major issue is the extent to which we can generalize about cultures in terms of social systems constructed out of reconstructed dispositions. Building on foundations laid by Émile Durkheim's functionalist sociological approach, many people have sought to capture these coherent systems on the basis of a handful of texts. But the reality of these systems is often difficult to pin down—too often we are dealing with fragmentary or idiosyncratic perspectives on a narrow range of social issues, which means that the generalizations are not necessarily fully representative of the past societies under analysis. It really depends on how critically we use our constructions—are they "tools for thinking with" or are they our finalized statements about past realities?

These are questions worth bearing in mind as we turn to the paradigm-creating work of Peter Brown. Brown gave form and voice to the idea of *The World of Late Antiquity* (1971) as a distinctive period in its own right, stretching from the late Roman Empire to the Arab conquests of the seventh century and a little beyond. At the heart of his vision of the period lay an appreciation of the sophistication and evolution of complex cultural worlds, an appreciation which grew over time through an alliance with the more sociological and anthropological thought of Mary Douglas and Ernst Gellner. In one of his most famous early studies, he used Syrian hagiography to sketch the social functions and values of enigmatic holy men such as Symeon Stylites, who consciously developed their charisma as marginal figures capable of resolving differences and providing spiritual leadership outside standard institutional parameters.[14] The combination of functionalism and evocative storytelling also characterized his published lectures on the cults of saints, in which he used hagiographical sources to rescue an appreciation of the role of cultic activities in social processes from the more pessimistic critiques of Delehaye and others.[15] All in all, the saints themselves mattered less than what they revealed about how late-antique society worked.

The importance of sociological and anthropological observations within studies of saints, sanctity, and cults is rarely missed. The 1980s saw the publication of three landmark volumes on this front that opened up cross-cultural perspectives across different Christianities and into Islam, Judaism, and Buddhism: Donald Weinstein and Rudolph Bell's *Saints and Society* (1982), the Stephen Wilson-edited *Saints and their Cults* (1985), and *Sainthood: Its Manifestations in World Religions* (1988), edited by Richard Kieckhefer and George Bond. From there, the habits of thinking about saints as universal social constructs quickly became second nature. One might barely blink to find engaged talk about charisma, "cultural markets," or "creative consumptions" in

Aviad Kleinberg's *Flesh Made Word: Saints' Stories and the Western Imagination* (2008). Indeed, such has been the success of the sociological turn in studies of late-antique and early-medieval saints that Fenella Cannell, in the excellent 2006 collection *The Anthropology of Christianity*, suggested that anthropologists look to the studies of Peter Brown and Judith Herrin for inspiration about how to pursue socially-grounded investigations of religious cultures. History does not have to be full of overt fussing about models and jargon to be exemplary in its methodologies—as long, that is, as its practitioners remain engaged with potential collaborators in relevant disciplines or departments.

One should, nevertheless, take care with some of Brown's models, just as one should never believe in any model too much. One criticism often levelled at his work is that there is not often a lot of meticulous source criticism on display. This is not to say that Brown was naïve in what he was attempting to do with the saints' Lives he used. Indeed, like Graus, he was seeking to understand the worlds conjured up in the round, including their imaginative spaces. He was alive to the variability in attitudes displayed in his texts and, particularly in his later work, would provide a multiplicity of overlapping or competing sketches of individual writers negotiating the shifting cultural contours of the evolving "micro-Christendoms." One suspects also that, like many other great historians, he did not want the tedious mechanisms of source criticism and historiographical reflection to get in the way of the telling of a really good story. His treatment of St. Radegund of Poitiers (d. 587) in *The Rise of Western Christendom* (1st ed. 1996; 3rd ed. 2013) illustrates this well. Brown's purpose in writing about Radegund was to highlight how "a woman's piety could act as a bridge between the new barbarian, military elites of northern Gaul and what had previously been a largely 'Roman' form of religion, cultivated by the leisured and still largely civilian elites of the south" (228). The account that follows catalogues key examples of the saint's "intense, melodramatic piety," drawing on the two *vitae* by Venantius Fortunatus and Baudovinia, with added details from Gregory of Tours' *Histories*. At no point, however, is anything made of the significant differences between the sources and their projections of different kinds of female sanctity—the story is told to substantiate a kind of piety, not to make claims about Radegund herself or her historians. For any comment on the hagiography itself, one must look elsewhere.[16]

Hagiography as a source for social history has been important to understanding the experiences of women such as Radegund. Indeed, as Jane Schulenburg observed, there is no other kind of source for the early Middle Ages in which the lives and experiences of women are so central.[17] This is as true for Byzantium or Ireland as it is for the English or Frankish kingdoms, with growing literatures dedicated to each. One can usefully compare Suzanne Wemple's approach in her 1981 study *Women in Frankish Society* to Schulenburg's *Forgetful of their Sex* (1998) to get a sense of development. Wemple proceeded predominantly from legal sources and chronicles, with hagiography only introduced cautiously to aid with discussions about ideals of chastity and a few other issues. Schulenberg, in contrast, opened her study by defending a more systematic use of hagiography about women—both for identifying patterns and changes in ideals, and for finding the "incidental details" which hinted at authentic reportage. Bringing hagiography to the centre here was explicitly not to be at the expense of studying non-hagiographical sources to provide historical anchors. Indeed, efforts to focus excessively on hagiography elsewhere to sketch an unanchored, long view of women's experiences transcending history have not met with much success or critical acclaim.[18]

More controversial has been the idea that there was a specifically female hagiographical discourse that developed in Merovingian Gaul. A broad analysis of the issue is obscured not least by the fact that many hagiographies circulated without any indication of who wrote them, so female authorship cannot easily be ruled out (or, perhaps, it is ruled out more often than it ought to be). In such a restricted field, two accounts of St. Radegund became the focal point for debate because one was known to be written by the male hagiographer and panegyrist Venantius Fortunatus, while the other was written by the nun Baudovinia, both contemporaries of Radegund's in Poitiers. It had already been argued by Étienne Delaruelle in 1953 that the two accounts represented different models of sanctity, one more private, the other more public. Wemple pushed this further with the claim that Baudovinia "was the first [hagiographer] to emphasize typically female attributes" for a saint, a novelty generated by her apparently unusual position in the period as a woman writing about another woman (*Women in Frankish Society*, 183–84).[19] These attributes include emotion, concern for peace, and charity. But whether these were intended to be distinctly feminine virtues remains an open question: "no conventions for the writing of female hagiography emerged," as Julia Smith observed, while John Kitchen identified plenty of points of comparison between Baudovinia's Radegund and male saints.[20] The nature of female sanctity was an issue, but the resources employed by medieval hagiographers to understand it were firmly rooted in male or universal hagiographical discourses.

Issues of sex and gender are crucial elements in transforming late-antique and early-medieval histories so that they are more than just accounts of state formation and kingship, and more than the great deeds of rich white men. Related and essential moves have seen hagiography used to explore other "margins" of the medieval world, such as ethnic, religious, and social differences and the monstrous. (The term "margins" can, of course, be read as marginalizing itself, and one may often want to think in terms of alternative centres of power and discourse.) This leads us to the influences, directly and indirectly, of theorists such as Derrida and Foucault who encouraged such de-centring—and who in the process encouraged greater attention to narrative.

For many medievalists, after Derrida and Foucault, the crucial theorist is narratologist Hayden White. A medievalist by training, White argued that, while there may be historical facts the truth of which cannot be denied, all efforts to present or talk about those facts are acts of interpretation.[21] From this perspective, all narratives are essentially subjective—although this is not to say that nothing is ever true, despite claims to the contrary by both supporters and critics of White. There are facts—he is clear about that—but the status and interpretation of those facts may differ. Postmodernism is not a licence to make everything up. Nevertheless, here we are not far away from Derrida's maxim "il n'y a pas de hors-texte" (there is no outside-text), a claim that reality and language never truly intersect.[22] For many medievalists this is largely unproblematic, because we know that we are locked into partial views of textual discourses with no possibility of external validation (subject to the invention of time travel, of course). Indeed, we have already seen Geary's dismissal of the idea that Derrida announced something new here, because Delehaye, Graus, and many more had already explored issues about textuality and truth. Geary, building on thoughts by Gabrielle Spiegel, even wondered if manuscripts could help to supply something like the "outside-text" that would lead to a better appreciation of the social logic of the text.[23] In the meantime, however, White's ideas did have a subtle and important effect on raising the methodological game.

An interesting study in this context is Ian Wood's *The Missionary Life* (2001), an exploration of "hagiography about mission." Wood's point of departure was to extend methodological insights brought into focus by Walter Goffart's 1988 magnum opus, *The Narrators of Barbarian History*; indeed, Wood's students in Vienna labelled the preparatory lectures *The Narrators of Missionary History* (xi). Goffart, having read White, had taken on board the not-so-postmodern lesson that our narrative source material is a tapestry of "textual arguments," in which the past is shaped by authors to fulfil particular functions, which themselves are a reconstructable part of that past. We are only so far from Charles Jones here. One important case study concerned Bede's representations of St. Wilfrid of York in the *Ecclesiastical History of the English People* (731/4), which Goffart maintained systematically downplayed many of the achievements Stephanus of Ripon had claimed for the bishop, for instance by asserting that John of Beverley rather than Wilfrid had introduced Roman liturgical song to Northumbria. The arguments of Stephanus and Bede about Wilfrid limited what could be reconstructed about Wilfrid in real life, but the reward was that we potentially knew more about the worlds of the authors. Wood applied this kind of insight to the study of hagiographical accounts of missionary work in the period ca. 700 to ca. 1000, recasting the story of the spread of Christianity in northern Europe into a fractured series of debates between groups about the meaning of the recent missionary past. Who converted Bavaria, for instance, became a burning issue as eighth-century churchmen used the past to articulate the parameters of their authority and capture something of the muscular aristocratic culture in which they lived.

For now, at least, the textual dimensions of hagiography have expanded and refined the ways in which historians interrogate narrative sources. Ideas, arguments, and structures have their place alongside simple action in the historical canon. The influences of philology, sociology, and postmodernism mean that we are now better-placed to use hagiography as something more sophisticated than an account of the past to be considered simply for whether or not it is true and what it says about religion. It is a valuable cultural artefact in its own right that reveals much about the world of the people who created it in many forms.

The Tensions of Total History and Comparative History

A necessary nuancing of the above views can be found in what we might call the "total history" approach. The point, for Spiegel and Geary, of looking for context was to understand "the social logic of the text." The more context one establishes, the more one can understand the intended meanings of a text and, if one is lucky, its reception. Analysis, here, relies on establishing coherence within a given situation or cluster of related situations. The role models were already there, even if they lacked some of the polemical framing. Poulin's 1975 study of hagiography and society in Carolingian Aquitaine could be seen in this light, as the author explicitly set out to provide a case study to aid comparative work. In 1988, Máire Herbert published an exemplary study of hagiographical tradition in the Irish Columban *familia*, while Kenneth Baxter Wolf published one on Eulogius and his accounts of the ninth-century martyrs of Córdoba the same year. Thomas Head's much-praised study of hagiographical tradition and politics in the diocese of Orléans came out only two years later. A more recent high point has been Janneke Raaijmakers' study *The Making of the Monastic Community of Fulda* (2012), which explored changing monastic identity through a series of hagiographies, contextualized by evidence from archaeology, charters, histories, and memorial notes. I remember leading Carolingianist Mayke de Jong introducing her then-future Utrecht colleague Raaijmakers at a conference and noting how, once, one filleted hagiography for the specific religious or social points one needed to address a research theme, but now one had to understand everything.

It is not possible, sadly, to contextualize every early medieval saint's Life as thickly as Raaijmakers was able to do for those produced at Fulda in the ninth century. Either the contextual evidence is missing or else the texts are difficult to pin down in time and space. Even a rich case study such as Fulda has gaps (in this case, many of its manuscripts were lost in the Thirty Years War). Sometimes the diversity of relevant expertise calls for a team instead, perhaps most roundedly exemplified by the 1989 collection of essays on the cult of St. Cuthbert edited by Bonner, Rollason, and Stancliffe, which covers aspects of art history, architecture, palaeography, cult, and hagiography. There are other routes the individual historian can take. One bold recent example is Jamie Kreiner's 2014 study of *The Social Life of Merovingian Hagiography*, in which she sought to contextualize stories and language regarding saints in relation to legal culture, political community, attitudes towards wealth, and attitudes towards holy places. Japanese opera, psychology, and narratology also get discussed en route. This enabled Kreiner to conclude that hagiographies were a successful part of contemporary political discourse—a perceptive claim as interesting for sounding like common sense in 2014 as it is for being a world away from how Krusch would have thought about the same material in 1914.

The necessary move towards deep context has not yet fully opened up sustained comparative histories. There are, after all, limits to the volume of data and scholarship any individual person can process and write up. Wolfert van Egmond's Dutch doctoral dissertation compared Auxerre, Utrecht, and Würzburg, but space restricted the published version *Conversing with the Saints* (2006) to Auxerre alone. Ian Wood's *The Missionary Life* (2001) stands as a leading example of the benefits of juxtaposing different focused case studies across time and space, as he followed missionary hagiography from the Rhineland eastwards. It still understandably leaves the question of how such material connected to or compared to saintly traditions elsewhere. We still have not mastered comparisons between Latin traditions, let alone worked out rules about how to compare Latin texts to Western vernacular texts or Eastern ones. Projects such as Philippart's multi-author *Hagiographies*, with introductions to individual areas, ought to provide the necessary building blocks to push forward here. Philippart has also worked on quantitative analyses of saint-types using databases and graphs—a useful application of technology to hagiology.[24] But there remain many barriers to comparisons, including linguistic competence and different historiographical traditions with their own conceptual repertoires. Too often, "comparison" has been pursued by juxtaposing essays on different topics, rather than getting scholars to engage directly with each other. There are exceptions.[25] Realistically, more co-authorship and teamed project work is needed.

And what if we leave a Christian context? If it is hard enough to compare Irish and Frankish hagiography, and unsettling to compare Latin and Greek, imagine the potential dissonance and joys of exploring accounts of Muslim or Buddhist people whose special lives became exemplars. Biographies of Muhammad offer a distinctive blend of oral tradition, exegesis, and literary quality that makes them highly controversial as histories.[26] They nevertheless reveal much about faith and conversion as expressed through example. The number of hagiographical digressions in early Tibetan Buddhist literature in the same period, following the region's conversion, suggests similar impulses there.[27] From China, there is a wealth of material such as the sixth-century *Biqiuni Zhuan* about nuns or the serial biographies of monks by Huijiao (d. 554), Daoxuan (d. 667), and Zanning (d. 1001), that lend themselves readily to discussions of how biographies reflect institutional attitudes to sex, diet, and asceticism.[28] There are many points of connection.

The crucial issue is: what difference does comparison make? There is no point in engaging with such studies simply to be fashionable and to revel in a bit of orientalist exoticism. But politically, culturally, the world needs more culturally diverse and challenging histories, not just retreads of nineteenth-century nationalist fantasies. There are clearly some intriguing universals in play that help historians to reach beyond familiar confines. To pick a significant one: what "historical" means is endlessly malleable in the face of belief, literary forms, and politics. Superficial formal similarities in holy biographies across cultures allow for some systematic analysis that would enable clearer appreciation of how that works, while also forcing those who write and read about the medieval West to engage with different epistemological schemes.[29] Sometimes you do not fully appreciate your assumptions until you have had to step away from what seems comfortable. Not that there are not comfortable things: one could have enriching conversations about what different hagiographies reveal about processes of institutional memory, or about reinforcing and recreating gender roles, or about where institutional religion and government do or do not intersect. One could even reopen the debate about what hagiography actually is, if it makes sense as a concept to people in or working on religious cultures that are not Christian. Sometimes such investigations do not add very much to the conversation. One will not know, however, until one has tried.

Conclusion: Have Questions and Be Critical

What does the history of studying saints' Lives suggest about appropriate methodologies? I promised at the beginning of the chapter not to be too prescriptive. The reason people still look back to the work of Delehaye or Krusch is partly because a lot of it does stand up to rigorous criticism and offers inspiration. That we have also had many productive conversations about why it is not perfect is great, because there is nothing worse than having a methodology so watertight that one never has to think about what one is doing and think of new ways to do things. I was once told a story about Canadian medievalist Paul Dutton suggesting at a conference that we can only really hope to find new ways to be wrong, rather than to be right, as most of our conclusions will get overturned eventually. Being wrong is not necessarily a problem; refusing to be a critical and reflective thinker is a problem. What we should do is go forward, be prepared to look into insights that might come from any methodology, but also be prepared to call it when the latest emperor has no clothes. Get good questions, and if they do not give you good answers, get better questions. Do not mistake methodology or fancy quotations from theorists for answers. Be critical.

There are still lingering issues about what questions and methods are fit for purpose. As Graus pointed out, we might try to put factual weight on statements in hagiographies that were never intended to bear that weight. We might remember Ermanrich of Ellwangen in Chapter 1; he believed that spiritual truths helped him to sidestep the problem of a paucity of evidence for the "historical" activities of St. Sualo. It is not as if "alternative facts" are a thing of the past—they are and were crucial to understanding all manner of processes; social, political, literary. To recognize that some people might see different truths (or truths differently) should not be to open the door to making up any old rubbish. But life is richer than a succession of things happening. To evaluate methods for studying hagiography, we need to be alive to the different kinds of truths people might seek.

Notes

[1] Hippolyte Delehaye, *The Work of the Bollandists through Three Centuries, 1615–1915* (Princeton: Princeton University Press, 1922); David Knowles, *Great Historical Enterprises: Problems in Monastic History* (London: Nelson, 1963). One can also find a short history at www.bollandistes.org.

[2] See preface to *Analecta Bollandiana* 1 (1882): 5–8.

[3] Patrick Geary, "Saints, Scholars, and Society: The Elusive Goal," in his *Living with the Dead in the Middle Ages* (Ithaca: Cornell University Press, 1994), 9–29 at 17.

[4] Richard Sharpe, *Medieval Irish Saints' Lives: An Introduction to Vitae Sanctorum Hiberniae* (Oxford: Oxford University Press, 1991), 80–81.

[5] On Krusch's efforts and their reception see Harry Breslau, *Geschichte der Monumenta Germaniae Historica* (Hannover: Hahn, 1921), 654–57.

[6] Bruno Krusch, "Zur Florians- und Lupus-Legende. Eine Entgegnung," *Neues Archiv der Gesellschaft für ältere deutsche Geschichtskunde* 24 (1899): 533–70 at 559.

[7] Pascale Bourgain, "Gregory of Tours' Works: Manuscripts, Language, and Style," in *A Companion to Gregory of Tours*, ed. Alexander Callander Murray (Leiden: Brill, 2013), 141–89.

[8] Daniel König, "Wilhelm Levison und die Missionsgeschichte im Spiegel der Hagiographie," in *Wilhelm Levison (1876–1947): Ein jüdisches Forscherleben zwischen wissenschaftlicher Anerkennung und politischem Exil*, ed. Matthias Becher and Yitzhak Hen (Siegburg: Schmitt, 2010), 33–53.

[9] Bertram Colgrave, *The Earliest Saints' Lives Written in England* (London: Oxford University Press, 1959).

[10] *Bede and his World: The Jarrow Lectures, 1958–1993*, ed. Michael Lapidge (Aldershot: Variorum, 1994).

[11] Hans-Jörg Gilomen, "Zum mediävistischen Werk von František Graus," *Basler Zeitschrift für Geschichte und Altertumskunde*, 90 (1989): 5–22.

[12] See further Baudouin de Gaiffier, "Mentalité de l'hagiographie médiéval, d'après quelques travaux récents," *Analecta Bollandiana* 86 (1968): 391–99 and *Mentalitäten im Mittelalter: Methodische und inhaltliche Probleme*, ed. František Graus (Sigmaringen: Thorbecke, 1987).

[13] Karl Bosl, "Der 'Adelheiligen.' Idealtypus und Wirklichkeit, Gesellschaft und Kultur im merowingerzeitlichen Bayern des 7. und 8. Jahrhunderts. Gesellschaftliche Beiträge zu den Viten der bayerischen Stammesheiligen Emmeram, Rupert, Korbinian," in *Speculum Historiale: Geschichte im Spiegel von Geschichtsschreibung und Geschichtsdeutung*, ed. Clemens Bauer, Laetitia Boehm, and Max Müller (Freiburg: Alber, 1965), 167–87.

[14] Brown, "The Rise and Function of the Holy Man in Late Antiquity."

[15] Brown, *The Cult of the Saints*.

[16] Brown's footnotes do not help much here, citing on the text only Brian Brennan, "St Radegund and the Early Development of her Cult at Poitiers," *Journal of Religious History* 13 (1985): 340–54. One might see now John Kitchen, *Saints' Lives and the Rhetoric of Gender: Male and Female in Merovingian Hagiography* (Oxford: Oxford University Press, 1998), 115–53, and Julia Smith, "Radegundis Peccatrix: Authorizations of Virginity in Late Antique Gaul," *Transformations of Late Antiquity*, ed. Philip Rousseau and Manolis Papoutsakis (Aldershot: Ashgate, 2009), 303–26, the latter a tribute to Brown.

[17] Jane Tibbets Schulenburg, *Forgetful of their Sex: Female Sanctity and Society 500–1100* (Chicago: Chicago University Press, 1998), chap. 1, originally "Saints' Lives as a Source for the History of Women, 500–1100," in *Medieval Women and the Sources of Medieval History*, ed. Joel Rosenthal (Athens: University of Georgia Press, 1990), 285–320.

[18] See the criticism of Lisa Bitel, *Land of Women: Tales of Sex and Gender from Early Ireland* (Ithaca: Cornell University Press, 1997) in C. Peyroux, "Lands of Women? Writing the History of Early Medieval Women in Ireland and Europe," in *Early Medieval Europe* 7 (1998): 217–27.

[19] Suzanne Wemple, *Women in Frankish Society: Marriage and the Cloister, 500 to 900* (Philadelphia: University of Pennsylvania Press, 1981), 183–84.

[20] Julia Smith, "The Problem of Female Sanctity in Carolingian Europe c. 780–920," *Past & Present* 146 (1995): 3–37, quote from 17.

[21] Hayden White, *The Content of the Form: Narrative Discourse and Historical Representation* (Baltimore: Johns Hopkins University Press, 1987).

[22] Jacques Derrida, *Of Grammatology*, trans. Gayatri Spivak (Baltimore: Johns Hopkins University Press, 1967), 158.

[23] Geary, "Saints," 18–22; Gabrielle Spiegel, "History, Historicism and the Social Logic of Text in the Middle Ages," *Speculum* 65 (1990): 59–86.

[24] Guy Philippart with Michel Trigalet, "Latin Hagiography Before the Ninth Century: A Synoptic View," in *The Long Morning of the Middle Ages*, ed. J. Davis and M. McCormick (Aldershot: Ashgate, 2008), 111–30.

[25] For one recent, later example, see Massimo Rondolino, *Cross-Cultural Perspectives on Hagiographical Strategies: A Comparative Study of the Standard Lives of St Francis and Milarepa* (London: Routledge, 2017).

[26] Andreas Görke, Harald Motzki, and Gregor Schoeler, "First Century Sources for the Life of Muhammad? A Debate," *Der Islam* 89 (2012): 2–59.

[27] Matthew Kapstein, *The Tibetan Assimilation of Buddhism: Conversion, Contestation, and Memory* (Oxford: Oxford University Press, 2000).

[28] Kieschnick, *The Eminent Monk*.

[29] William Gallois, *Time, Religion and History* (London: Routledge, 2007) is a useful general starting point if you want to see how it might work.

Chapter 4

Hagiographies and Early Medieval History

By way of a conclusion, this chapter turns its attention outwards to ask how hagiographical sources can be used in the study of Late Antiquity and the early Middle Ages, and indeed change how we see those periods. In a relatively compact book such as this, one cannot be exhaustive, so I have chosen to sketch some ways in which hagiography has or could shed light on some of the "big issues" of early medieval studies in the West—issues that shaped our views and misconceptions about that past. As we saw in Chapter 3, historians have used saints' Lives and related texts more in pursuit of some ends than others: understanding gender, for instance, rather than analyzing legal structures. Hagiographical evidence does offer distinctive takes on many issues, representing issues of morality and power processed relative to local politics, local cultural sensitivities, and expectations about narratives. Once, historians saw the period 500 to 900 as little more than an anarchic and simplistic "Dark Age" of misogyny, relative cultural and ethnic homogeneity, illiteracy, superstition, religious oppression, and limited horizons and travel, that all firmly brought an end to the progress of the progressive, multicultural civilization under the Romans for a millennium. That, of course, is often how the period is still seen in the media and in conservative polemics. And maybe it was often like that. But one must embrace all the available evidence, not just the parts that support existing prejudices, and there, hagiography reports worlds that are much richer and more complex than the tired "Dark Age" tropes might suggest. They might also pose new questions and open up new fields of inquiry altogether. We need to ask what difference hagiography makes to the Middle Ages.

In what follows, there are two important methodological issues to bear in mind. First, given everything we have seen in Chapters 1 to 3, we should remember all the issues of composition, circulation, and interpretation that mean we cannot use hagiographical narratives as unproblematic representations of past events "as long as we are careful." Most people know this, but it is always worth repeating. The second issue is simply that I will try to highlight some differences and similarities in emphasis and approach across time and space, in order to push further the underlying concern throughout this book: to contribute to stronger foundations for comparative histories using hagiographies.

The End of Civilization?

Let's start with one of the biggest questions of the period: did the fall of the western Roman Empire in the fifth century mean a catastrophic collapse of civilization and the beginning of a "Dark Age"? It is an old question that still causes disquiet, as it seems *prima facie* impossible that a sophisticated and complex empire could break up into smaller units, while experiencing seismic social changes through migration, land reorganization, and religious change, and it not be a disaster. Certainly, if one privileges quality artisanal production and robust state structures—never entirely unreasonable as yardsticks—one might see stark changes that are hard to gloss positively.[1] Most contemporary chronicles reflect anxiety and unrest. Unquestionably, many people died. (Technically: everybody.) But one might also find narratives that do not fit a "decline and fall" model, if one focuses on the successes of the successor kingdoms, the growing sophistication and wealth of the Church, or the changing role of the household. Hagiography offers distinctive material to help us investigate these issues.

Two related areas of interest that do not necessarily fit a "decline and fall" model are education and cultural production. Many historians have maintained, and still maintain, that standards of learning collapsed with the erosion of political institutions and the growing role of churches and monasteries in education in place of secular schools. But Pierre Riché, in *Éducation et culture dans l'occident barbare* (1962, 3rd edition translated by John Contreni as *Education and Culture in the Barbarian West* in 1975), showed long ago that such arguments significantly underestimated the vitality of the period and the nature of a Christian syllabus. Michael Wallace-Hadrill reminds us that "textual anarchy has nothing to do with spiritual decadence."[2] Work by Jacques Fontaine and, more recently, Yitzhak Hen in 2006's *Roman Barbarians* has strengthened this view and fed into more complex understandings of cultural production as power—something long recognized for the Carolingian period, thanks mainly to Rosamond McKitterick's studies, such as *The Carolingians and the Written Word* in 1989. And if knowledge is power, then the production of hagiography ought to reveal something about the workings of power in the period. Indeed, if one of the crucial dynamics involved in the transformation of the Roman world was a shift in the localized experiences of power, as some have suggested, then the localized perspectives of hagiography might be revealing.

An oft-cited piece of evidence here is Eugippius's (d. ca. 535) *Life of Severinus of Noricum*, which seems to provide a clear statement about the anxiety of the period. Within the first four chapters alone, we are told that "confusion reigned" under Attila the Hun, and that the people of Comegena on the Danube struggled against besieging armies, famine, and robbers. Severinus himself, his background uncertain, walks through this violent and unsettled world as an Old Testament-style prophet, providing a divinely inspired meta-commentary by liberating slaves, negotiating with kings to secure peace, and healing the blind and the lame. But is it, as Ward-Perkins suggested in his *The Fall of Rome and the End of Civilisation* in 2005, a fair reflection of perilous times or, as Friedrich Lotter suggested in his 1976 study *Severinus von Noricum*, a tapestry of literary motifs? One does not necessarily preclude the other. Both views, however, highlight that a real response to a perceived crisis was to sit down and write something complicated about it. Given the volume of hagiographical production in the period ca. 500–700, one might almost conclude that saints were pivotal in such change or that they were useful "people for thinking with" as people sought to understand the world around them.

One would not necessarily turn to hagiography for an optimistic view of history in the context of crisis. Both the Old and the New Testament often revolved around the theme of a limited elect group struggling against assaults of some sort. Saints' cults and literature about martyrs and confessors extended the relevance of the theme to new times and places. As the role model *par excellence* in Gaul, St. Martin had to struggle with the world around him to achieve anything. Even then, Sulpicius expected little longevity for Martin's successes, as he believed the end of the world was fast approaching. Hagiography in the sixth and seventh centuries looked back with a kind of nostalgia to those who had struggled against persecution, and cast new figures such as Leudegar (d. 679) as martyrs when it seemed forced given that they had died for political reasons. Often the past was retold to fit particular predetermined literary or theological schemes.

Many groups found biographies about holy people useful in their efforts to take new advantages. Constantius's *Life of Germanus of Auxerre* (written ca. 480), to take just one example, contributed to a blending of the values of senatorial aristocracy and Christian sanctity as much as Germanus himself had done. The author, himself possibly an aristocrat with an administrative position rather than a cleric, produced his work for a limited social circle surrounding Bishop Patiens of Lyon to provide a model for good behaviour and orthodoxy.[3] Such an interpretation may sound a little bland, but Constantius and

Patiens were part of the generation of Gallo-Roman aristocrats who had to find new meaning and roles for their powerful families and institutions as the old Roman world was remoulded around new structures. Biographical forms lent themselves well to expressing this. Indeed, Martin Heinzelmann saw here part of the development of *Bischofsherrschaft*, episcopal lordship, by a senatorial class reasserting itself and redefining itself through the Church.[4] One might be led to exaggerate the extent of an "aristocratic Church" on the basis of this evidence, especially if one compares the legal sources. Stories about saints were still part of how values were negotiated within society.

Involvement in the Church was more than a simple power-grab for the Gallic aristocracy. For all the disruptive behaviour of the Goths evoked by the author of the *Life of Caesarius of Arles*, the hero refused to give up on founding a female monastic house for his blood sister Caesaria, so that they could renounce their earthly property and family together (bk. 1, chaps. 28 and 35). The breaking up of blood families and the creation of spiritual ones became something of a monastic and hagiographical trope.[5] The inevitable unsettling of socio-economic patterns could, here, lead to a more positive Christian lifestyle. In Peter Brown's book, *Through the Eye of a Needle* (2013), the hagiography produced in Arles provided telling illustrations of the ways in which wealth was being claimed for charitable and building works, where once more of it may have gone into the consumption of luxury goods (512). If a key indicator of the "fall of civilization" was the declining demand for said luxury goods, then the hagiography of Arles suggests some reasons why this happened, as money and energy was diverted to less worldly or ostentatious ends.

Another way of looking at the issue is to ask how many new beginnings and opportunities emerged from or alongside crisis. One should be careful here not to devalue actual crisis and horror by saying that some people benefited, as that is a game that never ends well. But what one sees in the examples of Caesarius and Germanus is an effort to build new communities and to improve standards. The story of Germanus is also famous because he was drawn into arguments about heresy in Britain at a time when communities in Britain and Ireland were being redefined after the withdrawal of the Roman army in 410 and Palladius's efforts to extend Christianity. With the end of one world, another usually came. And so it is important to turn, in the next section, to what kind of culture hagiography helped to develop.

A Common European Culture?

The early Middle Ages has long been a period in which historians have sought the origins of some kind of common European culture or identity—a project that has been more or less controversial depending on the underlying attitudes towards inclusion and exclusion. Precisely what kind of European culture historians seek depends significantly upon their interests. Rob Bartlett, in his 1993 classic *The Making of Europe*, argued that Europe became increasingly homogeneous between ca. 1000 and ca. 1300: this was partly because of the Christian expansion into northern and eastern lands, he maintained, and partly because of the emergence of universities, knights, and other things which simultaneously marked the period's creativity and created common frames of reference. Sixty-one years earlier, as sinister nationalisms grew in popularity, Christopher Dawson published a very different *The Making of Europe*: for him, the crucial elements of a spiritual European unity, distinct from mere wealth or force, stemmed from Carolingian political expansion and the early spread of Christianity and Latin literacy into Germany before ca. 1000. There have, and will always be, different Europes to be made or broken in the imagination.

Saints and hagiography have their place in arguments about common cultures. In 1946, exiled in England from his native Germany, Wilhelm Levison wrote in *England and the Continent in the Eighth Century* about a Europe which had found its common ground in Christianity. Although he himself was Jewish, he saw that Christianity had provided shared ideas and social rhythms through the Bible and the liturgy. Saints were central to the formation of this culture because they were leading figures who spread it. As Levison's focus was Anglo-German relations, English saints Willibrord (d. 739) and Boniface (d. 754) were to the fore for working abroad, as were Alcuin (d. 804) and Charlemagne (d. 814) for devising a Christian Europe that transcended national identities a generation later. In 1954 Levison's former student, Theodor Schieffer, associated these enterprises with the "Foundations of Christian Europe" in his still-fundamental biography of Boniface.[6] This was not, of course, to claim that these saints had founded it all by themselves or completely; they had, however, played a lively and celebrated part in spreading ideas about religion, monasticism, and episcopal and papal authority. The sense of common cultural and religious ground, cutting across political divisions, was important. "Many of the noblest products of Western civilization," Levison argued, "have grown up from medieval foundations, from a common heritage which is even now a living reality among the individual nations in spite of their differences and their present struggles."[7]

It may not have struck Levison or Schieffer in quite this way, but hagiography was crucial to shaping the discourses involved. Boniface found inspiration for his behaviour in the stories of the martyrs travelling far and fighting for what they believed in.[8] When he died, many contemporaries immediately thought of comparisons with such saints. Willibald's *Life of Boniface* took the Englishman's achievements and "hagiographized" them for audiences across England, Gaul, Germany, and Tuscany (so he said), with inspiration from other texts, including Gregory the Great's *Dialogues*.[9] The work inspired more people to write hagiographies about the recent past, such as Arbeo of Freising (d. 784), who was keen to point out where Willibald was wrong. The work circulated outside Boniface's immediate spheres of operation to be copied alongside the classic "lives of the fathers," as we saw in Chapter 2. The long-term success of the "foundations of Christian Europe" Schieffer identified owed much to the fact that people from Wessex to Rome had shared ways of talking about holy behaviour through hagiographies.

There are many other ways to explore the idea that hagiography provided a shared way of imagining the active Christian life (and death). One could compare the way that Gregory's *Dialogues* inspired Adomnán of Iona and the anonymous author of the *Lives of the Fathers of Mérida* differently, the former as he wrote about one saint's many miracles in western Scotland, and the latter as he wrote about the trials of bishops in his town in Iberia. One could look at the ways in which the ascetic deserts of Egypt, so popularized in the West by Evagrius's *Life of Anthony*, were turned into "ocean deserts" in the tales of Columba and Brendan the Navigator, marshy deserts in the story of hermit Guthlac of Crowland (d. 715), or woodland deserts in Sturm of Fulda's quest to find a site for a monastic retreat. One could ask why Merovingian Gaul produced so many stories about both old and new martyrs as people explored the violence of Christian stories, while neighbours in Ireland, England, and Spain preferred confessors, when martyrs' tales circulated widely. (One might also wonder how all these texts spread so widely if, as popular myth would have it, no one travelled much in the Middle Ages.)

One cannot overstress the point: saints were crucial building blocks in Christian universality. Peter Brown, in *The Rise of Western Christendom*, called Late Antiquity and the early Middle Ages a world of "micro-Christendoms," in which communities sought to define the universal nature of Christian belief for local audiences (15). This observation came from a wider study of how Christian culture manifested itself differently, from Irish penitential practice to Gallic conciliar activity. Building on the argument, we might add that many instances of hagiography were attempts to create and map such micro-Christendoms. A story might be about taking Christian practice to the political heart of a pagan world, as in Muirchú's story of the clash between St. Patrick and King Lóegaire (bk. 1, chaps. 15(14)–21). It could be about the tensions between family expectations and Christian devotion, as in the Laon-centred *Life of Sadalberga*. Or, more often, it could be about the establishment of churches, monasteries, or cult sites, providing the local origin legends that one did not always get in long-form chronicles. But many audiences demanded more than parochialism. Gregory of Tours' hagiographical works encompassed worlds from the Holy Land to his own diocese, just as many martyrologies did from Ireland to Italy. Stories of Eastern saints circulated widely in the West. For people to understand what it meant for their local saint to be a saint, it was helpful to know how their example and life compared to those of other saints throughout the world. Saints were often local figures but that did not mean that the horizons of cults or their communities were small.

Saints' stories transmitted more than ideas about what saints were, as we have seen throughout. They praised the ideals of chastity and discipline, alongside the rejection of earthly things. They gave examples of behaviour that reinforced points of canon law concerning marriage and work. They illustrated that charitable works were socially desirable. They encouraged literacy and careful study. Naturally, they reinforced the moral superiority of pious individuals over the entire social spectrum, from kings and queens to the poorest—interestingly, keeping open the possibility of critiquing immorality and loose behaviour wherever it may be found, so that no one was ever protected simply by their social or institutional standing. Hagiography was not unique here, as the Bible itself fulfilled similar functions, as did sermons. Nevertheless, hagiography provided common tools for shaping expectations and actions, which allowed Christians across the West to develop their micro-Christendoms within similar parameters.

A World Defined by Ethnic Discourse?

"Micro-Christendoms" are fascinating but they cannot be understood without taking into account a whole range of smaller-scale identities. A woman living by the Rhine at any point in our period could consider herself to be defined by being a Christian, by being an active part of a household or family, by gender, by speaking a Germanic language, by her allegiance to a particular king, or by ethnic identity.[10] How any of these might determine her behaviour would depend entirely on any given situation. The issue of identities has been absolutely central to the study of Rome's fall and after, first because it appealed to early modern discourses on the relative merits of Roman civilization and Teutonic steel, and later as a reaction against the worst excesses of nationalism and racism in the twentieth century.[11] Nevertheless, it has been strongly and repeatedly argued that people were no less obsessed with identity in the past, and that the politics of identity formation was a central motor for developments in the period. There were even ethnic histories, in different ways: Jordanes' *History of the Goths* (ca. 550), Isidore of Seville's *Origins of the Goths, Vandals and Suevi* (1st version after 619, 2nd version after 624), Bede's *Ecclesiastical History of the English People* (731/4), and Paul the Deacon's *History of the Lombards* (ca. 799)—although the extent to which the identities narrated are literary fictions has also proved controversial.[12]

On the subject of ethnic discourse, hagiographies provide a difficult body of evidence. The "ethnic histories" mentioned above are often king-centric and the authors let stories unfold over hundreds of years of migrations, battles, and other incidents. Hagiographies are simply more local and confined. The old *Life of Genovefa of Paris* illustrates the consequences of this well, as the author narrates some of the events in the unsettled mid-fifth century, but the central point of identity alongside the saint is the city of Paris itself—especially its citizens and its churches. The author does not give Genovefa an ethnic label, while Hunnish and Frankish identities are mentioned principally to clarify over whom Attila and Childeric I respectively were kings (chaps. 12 and 26). Ethnic discourse was not irrelevant to hagiographies, but it was not necessarily where the emphasis lay either.[13] Bede provides a good example: his interest in the ecclesiastical genesis of the English people is certainly evident in his

Life of Cuthbert (e.g., chap. 16) and *Lives of the Abbots*; it is, however, not a theme that is systematically developed within those texts in the same way that it was in his *Ecclesiastical History*. Religious, civic, and other local identities tended to be to the fore.

There are always exceptions. Some ninth-century Saxon hagiography placed discourses about ethnicity much more prominently. The situation of the Saxons within Christendom was no doubt unusual, as their conversion had followed drawn-out conflicts with their Christian Frankish neighbours, during which close associations were made between religion and identity.[14] In early rounds, English missionaries were involved as they believed their ancestors and those of the Saxons were related. Although this was mentioned in letters, hagiographical stories of the missions downplayed this ethnic angle to emphasize the universality of the Christian faith.[15] A century later, however, connections between ethnicity and mission became more important. The most striking illustration of this comes in the *Translation of St Alexander*, written in Fulda at least in part to promote miracles performed at the shrine of St. Alexander in Wildeshausen after his relics were transported there in 851.[16] The first part of the work is an ethnographic account of the Saxons by Rudolf of Fulda, largely derived from Tacitus's *Germania* (written ca. 100) and including a legend that claims that the Saxons migrated from Britain, inverting the older story that the English migrated to Britain from Saxony. The point of this, in the context of the new cult of St. Alexander, was to emphasize the spiritual progress of the Saxons and their dukes in particular, as Duke Waltbraht had sponsored the collection of the relics from Rome in the first place. Ethnic discourse could be part of hagiographic discourse, but it depended on the circumstances whether the author wanted to employ it in that way.

One dynamic that was absent in the relationship between hagiography and ethnicity was the modern idea of a national "patron saint." There are, nevertheless, plenty of examples of particular saints acting as special patrons of particular polities or ethnic groups.[17] Tirechán, in his collection on St.

Patrick, asserted that Patrick would intercede for all the Irish on Judgement Day. In a similar vein, the anonymous Whitby nun who wrote the *Life of Pope Gregory* claimed that Gregory would stand up on behalf of the English that same day. Claims such as these were not common in hagiography and indeed could be contested. English bishops did agree to a special veneration of Gregory at a council in 747, but alongside Augustine of Canterbury, a man never afforded a saint's Life. There was a move, that did not get far, to add St. Boniface to this short list, and many more people, from Bede to Æthelstan, the first king of all the English, preferred to think of St. Cuthbert of Lindisfarne as their special patron. In Gaul, the serial efforts to promote St. Martin of Tours gave him an elevated position over other popular saints in the Frankish world, although devotion was often a personal issue.

Hagiography helps us to shift focus to the other identities and fora for action that talk of ethnicity might obscure. We have already seen with Genovefa the importance of civic identities as natural counterparts to the ways that saints were rallying points for communities. Ecclesiastical and monastic identities fit here, too—perhaps more so, given how many hagiographies across the West employed the story of a saint to narrate the origins of a particular church or monastery. The importance of gender identities within the texts cannot be underestimated either, from Gerald of Aurillac agonizing over how Carolingian expectations of male aristocratic behaviour clashed with his personal piety to the extent that he hid his tonsure, to St. Burgundofara in the *Life of Columbanus* having to chastize abbots Romaricus and Amatus, "not in feminine manner but in a manly way," for being misled by the alleged heretic Agrestius (bk. 2, chap. 10). People took on a range of roles and identified with different kinds of institutions, all affecting how they might act.

Many aspects of hagiographical discourse hinge on a specifically Christian identity. It was commonplace in persecution trial literature that the saint would declare "ego Christianus sum" ("I am a Christian"), as happens in the

Suffering of Laurentius of Rome and the Gallic *Suffering of St Quentin*. The flip side of this was that pagans were the enemy of choice for many hagiographers, even if they had to exaggerate as Gregory the Great may have done with the Lombards, because this provided the clearest contrast with the Christians (*Dialogues*, bk. 3, chap. 28). Hagiography about mission thrived by appropriating the same themes of otherness and persecution. Heretics were also useful here as religious others who felt that they held the true centre ground—indeed, Audoin of Rouen (d. 686) claimed in the *Life of Eligius of Noyon* that it was better for a martyr to struggle, fighting against heresy in the Universal Church, than to sacrifice themselves challenging idols (bk. 1, chap. 34). Early medieval Christian identities usually came with a strong sense of what people were fighting for and what they were fighting against.

The idea of Christian identity is not, in some ways, as well-defined in modern scholarship as other identities. For an ethnic identity, one can readily reel off likely contingent determining factors, such as shared language, dress, origin stories, or law, around which identities could be negotiated. One could do this with Christian beliefs and practices, too, in order to assess what it meant for someone to exclaim "ego Christianus sum." The Bible, of course, would provide a shared treasure trove of stories; the Holy Trinity, a recognized cornerstone of theology; baptism, a ritual entry into the community; and Judgement Day, a universally agreed destination for earthly history. There remained plenty of space—perhaps too much, in some people's view—for differences in interpretation and emphasis, which necessitated effort to police (as we will see in the next section). There were also many ways in which issues could be made present to those who identified with them, in rituals, sermons, canon law and councils, and reading. Hagiography and the celebration of saints contributed here with case studies of women and men leading good Christian lives and struggling against those with low or alternative standards, all grounded in textual worlds constructed out of appropriate religious sensibilities.

Worlds of Reform

A recurring theme in hagiographies is conflict over religious standards. This is not because standards were necessarily low, whatever claims one might make here about "Dark Age" tropes with their superstitious masses and their oppressive monolithic Church. Until Judgement Day itself, Christians needed to be vigilant about standards, and it was a serious duty for pastors to correct and to emend the behaviour of their flocks. Those flocks also needed to be vigilant in case the standards of the pastors were not up to scratch and many were not slow to take action if that happened. Often, people could not agree about what any of those standards might involve. We often use the word "reform," although this can imply actions which were more innovative, co-ordinated, or even conscious than was often the case.[18] Church councils and letters often employed the rhetoric of "correction" (*correctio* and *emendatio*) and renewal as part of ongoing efforts to restate and clarify points of canon law. Monastic reformers could, unsurprisingly, employ similar language. Often, people exaggerated declines in discipline and moral standing—if everything was fine, where was the imperative to act? The effect was to give the impression of waves of reform. One can jump from Caesarius of Arles to Gregory the Great to Boniface to Benedict of Aniane, and for each find similar anxieties about decline regardless of the progress made. *Plus ça change* ...

Hagiography could play a crucial role in the processes of reform. We saw in Chapter 1 that many hagiographers sought to fictionalize lived examples of idealized behaviour and to do this in a way that "institutionalized" the charisma of the saint in their churches or monasteries. The focus on particular individuals and centres can make programmes of reform seem more coherent and more deliberate than they may have been in practice. A much-debated example is Ardo's *Life of Benedict of Aniane*, written around 822 (if genuine). In it, Ardo confidently portrays Benedict's work to improve monastic discipline under Charlemagne, and then how he built up a unified empire-wide set of monastic customs under Louis the Pious, announced in Aachen between 816 and 819. Aniane is even described as "head of the monasteries" (*caput cenobiorum*) for those other institutions in which people wanted to follow its practices. This was, however, not so much a network with a defined centre and plan of action as a way of articulating the monastery's (and Benedict's) inspirational status.[19] In practice, a principle of "unity within diversity" remained in place.

The languages of reform reinforced aspects of action, even if much was, unsurprisingly, cliché. Ardo talked about Benedict "correcting" the wicked and their customs (*mores*) when he was younger, and rooting out error when he was older at Aachen (chap. 2; chap. 46). Willibald described Boniface's councils as efforts to correct (*corrigere* and *emendare*) ecclesiastical and lay practices (*instituta*), as well as opportunities to end the "darkness" of heresies (chap. 7). There was, maybe, a penitential air to such talk, as many hagiographers used the same language to describe the importance of making amends after sin.[20] Reform as penitential discourse fit many moods of the early Middle Ages and was by no means restricted to specifically monastic contexts. Indeed, Peter Brown has argued that changes in penitential culture and related attitudes towards the afterlife in the seventh century marked a sharp divide between ancient and medieval Christianity more generally—change is not all about high politics and trade.[21] Change in penitential practice also prefigures the shift in the eighth century to what Anne-Marie Helvétius has called the enjoining of "canonical vengeance," in which people relied increasingly on punishment to police change alongside discussions and decisions at councils.[22] What better way to illustrate such ideas than through the exemplary stories of the saints and their enemies?

Hagiography, as mentioned above, takes us into a world of reform that emphasizes local situation and individual agency. Again, the sixth-century *Life of Caesarius of Arles* illustrates this well. Its classic tale of an exemplary bishop and holy man unfolds with the hero selflessly providing leadership to inspire and correct the behaviour of his fellow bishops to build a new Christian world: "he motivated some with sweet speech and terrified others with encouragement, some he corrected with threats, others with encouragement, some he restrained from vices through love, others through threat of punishment; he warned some in a general sense through proverbs, and reproached others more harshly by calling God as a witness" (bk. 1, chap. 17). Hagiography about mission understandably has similar motifs throughout, as figures such as Willibrord or Anskar of Hamburg-Bremen confronted pagans and founded new Christian communities in northern Europe and then took this sense of vigour back to churches and councils elsewhere. Saints were epicentres of change and agitators for standards few could hope to meet.

Hagiography "and Society"?

Underlying some of the assumptions behind the discussions in this book is the central point about studying hagiography now: that it is a "social-historical" resource that takes us beyond the more familiar worlds of kings and their wars. For many historians in the twenty-first century, history as a discipline remains predominantly about the study of power, and that means focusing on the richest and most culturally advantaged. There is, naturally, much fodder for such studies in hagiographies: courts are the scenes for important events, from the Irish *Life of Molua*'s infamous account of improving the quality of beer at a feast using a saint's shoe (chap. 50)[23] to Rimbert's *Life of Anskar of Hamburg-Bremen*'s mannered discussions of mission and high politics in Francia and Sweden. But one of the joys of hagiography is that it often concerns the margins and "ordinary lives," either as literary motifs or historical asides—the dealings of families, farmers, merchants, and anyone else who might not immediately catch the eye of a chronicler.

The extent to which one might gain access to "ordinary lives" (literary or historical) is often limited, but it is there. Gregory of Tours' four books on the miracles of St. Martin provide early examples of people afflicted with ill health (mostly blindness or some form of paralysis), people working fields, even the attraction of stealing bees for honey. The golden age of such lists of miracles was the ninth century, with its famous accounts of the viking-plagued wandering monks of St. Philibert's of Noirmoutier, the similarly troubled carers of St. Germanus in Paris, and the vaguely competitive stories in Saxony celebrating the power of the cults of Liudger of Münster, Willehad of Bremen, Alexander at Wildeshausen, and St. Vitus at Corvey. As they were for Gregory, most of the beneficiaries of miracles were ordinary people, often afflicted by ill-health, and many having committed some kind of sin, ranging in Altfrid's *Life of Liudger* alone from people who had entered uncanonical marriages to a man called Adam who wandered from shrine to shrine seeking redemption and freedom from chains after he had killed his brother, Henry. These stories all provide rich material for histories of marriage and sex, histories of healthcare, histories of food, and histories of law.

Many stories take place within households otherwise rarely encountered. Take the Roman *gesta martyrum* and related texts such as the *Deeds of Xystus*: they often revolve around tensions within a household of extended family and serving staff—tensions surrounding conversion, tensions surrounding grants to churches and inheritances, tensions surrounding marriage and sex.[24] Latin Christendom does not make much sense without seeing how such things affected the organization, moral codings, and financial basis of lived Christianity.

Economic issues arise in the texts, too, although often incidentally. We see this in the way the *Life of Brigit* and *Life of Columbanus* have multiple stories about crafts and harvests. We see it in the way people devote money to support Christian activities, such as the time the Frisian merchant Ibbo gave himself and his wealth to support Maximin of Trier, or in Caesarius of Arles' liberation of slaves. Long-distance mercantile travels underpinned much of the long pilgrimage narrative of Willibald of Eichstätt as he negotiated his way from England to the Holy Land via Rome. There was always anxiety about the accumulation of wealth, from St. Anthony giving away his riches to live among God's poor to Balthild being warned in a vision (oddly, not hers) against wearing jewellery after her monastic enclosure. St. Columba would not even accept a rich gift from one patron until the benefactor repented of the sin of avarice (bk. 1, chap. 50). Economic factors were an inevitable part of the hagiographical world—and, at the same time, hagiography sought to influence economic behaviour. An economic historian who dismisses hagiographies as monkish religious fantasy is missing out.

Finally, many of the issues raised about ordinary lives sit uneasily with classic caricatures of the early Middle Ages. Relative social mobility was real and can be studied with the aid of hagiography.[25] People travelled great distances to far-off lands without it necessarily being particularly remarkable. They are slow to believe anything they are told without some kind of proof. Women are important social actors in their own right. There is no shortage of order and justice, with arbitrary violence relatively contained. People may often have been oppressed, but many were also terrible at doing what they were told by kings, churchmen, their mothers, or anyone—especially saints. It is hardly an idyllic pastoral Middle Ages but it is hardly barbaric and simple either. Hagiography, for all its reputation as a literature of the superstitious, does not allow for a simple affirmation of the tropes about the "Dark Ages."

Conclusion: There is Work to Be Done

Hagiography, in the end, can be seen to have made differences to early medieval history on two fronts. First, by writing about saints in various ways, hagiographers inadvertently provided stories that expose the diversity and complexity of early medieval society in matters of literature, politics, sex, wealth, and organization, all with perspectives often quite different to those found in chronicles, legal documents, or other sources. Second, hagiography itself was part of those societies and the ways in which people sought to make them. It created common points of reference, fed into debates about morality and identity, and was generally used actively to encourage change rather than naïvely to record the early medieval world. Historians who have neglected hagiography (if there are many left) have missed rich resources that speak to emerging fields such as medical humanities while unsettling the old certainties about the period.

Even for historians who have taken hagiography seriously, there are new avenues available for exploration, as we have seen. The commonalities of hagiography provide a good starting point for exploring differences across the period in new and productive ways. Sometimes this will involve studying the same literary motifs employed differently to see, for instance, how Ireland and Egypt worked. One might also seize on how the importance of ethnic identities and *translationes* in ninth-century Saxony is distinctive and speaks to its unusual situation post-conquest. So, too, the popularity of hagiography about mission a century earlier says much about community-building and the expansion of Christendom, and it forms an interesting contrast with the stories of martyrs and confessors popular in older Christian centres to the south and east a generation earlier. Hagiography was varied, situationally meaningful, and can provide useful framings for comparative histories.

A short-term goal here is to open up better conversations between scholars working on Latin traditions and those working on sacred biographies from other traditions. This means not just more collections of essays in which there is only juxtaposition, but individual and collaborative work in which actual comparison is made. If we cannot talk about a single Latin tradition, we will need to be judicious in selections for comparison. The relationship between monastic settings and institutional memories might, for instance, make for a profitable comparison between sixth-century texts *Lives of the Jura Fathers*, Cyril of Scythopolis's *Lives of the Palestinian Monks*, and Hui Jiao's *Lives of Eminent Monks*, but maybe Gregory of Tours and John of Ephesus were too publicly active to fit into the same bracket. There is plenty of scope to compare the situations in which biographical texts were rewritten. Comparing hagiographical reflections on the eighth-century conversions of Germania to Christianity and Tibet to Buddhism in the centuries that followed could be instructive. There will be literary and theological differences across the board, but it would be valuable to map what these are and to what extent they are meaningful and revealing.

Study of hagiography has, in short, been significant in shaping the way we see the Middle Ages. Hagiography has the potential to help take us further still, towards a better global understanding of the past worlds that remain fascinating and full of meaning for present audiences.

Notes

1 Bryan Ward-Perkins, *The Fall of Rome and the End of Civilization* (Oxford: Oxford University Press, 2005); Chris Wickham, *Framing the Early Middle Ages* (Oxford: Oxford University Press, 2005).

2 J. M. Wallace-Hadrill, *The Frankish Church* (Oxford: Clarendon Press, 1983), 121.

3 Wolfert van Egmond, *Conversing with the Saints: Communication in Pre-Carolingian Hagiography from Auxerre* (Turnhout: Brepols, 2006), 26–36.

4 Martin Heinzelmann, *Bischofsherrschaft in Gallien* (Zurich: Artemis, 1976).

5 Lutz von Padberg, *Heilige und Familie. Studien zur Bedeutung familiengebundener Aspekte in den Viten des Verwandten- und Schülerkreises um Willibrord, Bonifatius und Liudger*, 2nd ed. (Mainz: Gesellschaft für mittelrheinische Kirchengeschichte, 1997).

6 Theodor Schieffer, *Winfrid-Bonifatius und die christliche Grundlegung Europas*, 2nd ed. (Darmstadt: Wissenschaftliche Buchhandlung, 1972).

7 Wilhelm Levison, *England and the Continent in the Eighth Century* (Oxford: Clarendon Press, 1946), 173.

8 James T. Palmer, "Martyrdom and the Rise of Missionary Hagiography in the Late Merovingian World," in *The Introduction of Christianity into the Early Medieval Insular World*, ed. Roy Flechner and Máire Ní Mhaonaigh (Turnhout: Brepols, 2016), 157–80.

[9] Ian Wood, *The Missionary Life: Saints and the Evangelisation of Europe 400–1050* (London: Routledge, 2001), 57–64; James T. Palmer, *Anglo-Saxons in a Frankish World, 690–900* (Turnhout: Brepols, 2009).

[10] Julia M. H. Smith, "Did Women Have a Transformation of the Roman World?," *Gender & History* 12 (2000): 552–71.

[11] Patrick Geary, *The Myth of Nations: The Medieval Origins of Europe* (Princeton: Princeton University Press, 1999); Ian Wood, *The Modern Origins of the Early Middle Ages* (Oxford: Oxford University Press, 2013).

[12] Walter Goffart, *The Narrators of Barbarian History (AD550–800): Jordanes, Gregory of Tours, Bede, and Paul the Deacon* (Princeton: Princeton University Press, 1988). The 2005 reprint contains a new preface with Goffart's tetchy reflections on how his book was received.

[13] Jamie Kreiner, *The Social Life of Merovingian Hagiography* (Cambridge: Cambridge University Press, 2014), 132–36.

[14] Robert Flierman, *Saxon Identities, AD150–900* (London: Bloomsbury, 2017), chaps. 4 and 5.

[15] Palmer, *Anglo-Saxons in a Frankish World*, 53–59.

[16] Philippe Depreux, "La sublimation de la soumission des Saxons au pouvoir franc et la translation de saint Alexandre de Rome à Wildeshausen (851)," in *Faire l'événement au Moyen Âge*, ed. Claude Carozzi and Huguette Taviani-Carozzi (Aix-en-Provence: Publications de l'Université de Provence, 2007), 219–34.

[17] Alan Thacker, "Pecularis patronus noster: The Saint as Patron of the State in the Early Middle Ages," in *The Medieval State*, ed. J. R. Maddicott and David Palliser (London: Hambledon, 2000), 1–24.

[18] Steven Vanderputten, *Monastic Reform as Process: Realities and Representations in Medieval Flanders, 900–1100* (Ithaca: Cornell University Press, 2013). On the problem of language, see Julia Barrow, "Ideas and Applications of Reform," in *The Cambridge History of Christianity* 3, ed. T. F. X. Noble and J. M. H. Smith (Cambridge: Cambridge University Press, 2008), 345–62.

[19] Walter Ketteman, *Subsidia Anianense: Überlieferungs- und textgeschichtliche Untersuchungen zur Geschichte Witiza-Benedikts, seines Klosters Aniane und zur sogenannten "anianischen Reform"* (unpublished dissertation, Universität Duisburg-Essen), 127 (http://duepublico.uni-duisburg-essen.de/servlets/DocumentServlet?id=18245).

[20] Adomnán, *Vita Columbae*, bk. 1, chap. 50; *Passio Leudegarii*, chap. 37; *Visio Baronti*, chap. 2; *Passio Kiliani*, chap. 13.

[21] Peter Brown, *The Ransom of the Soul: Afterlife and Wealth in Early Western Christianity* (Cambridge, MA: Harvard University Press, 2015), esp. 211.

[22] At a conference on *The Languages of Reform* in York in January 2017.

[23] The full text can be found in *Vitae sanctorum Hiberniae*, ed. Heist, 131–45.

[24] Kristina Sessa, "Domestic Conversions: Households and Bishops in Late Antique Papal Legends," in *Religion, Dynasty, and Patronage*, ed. Cooper and Hillner, 79–114.

[25] Allen Jones, *Social Mobility in Late Antique Gaul* (Cambridge: Cambridge University Press, 2009).

Further Reading

This lightly annotated guide to further reading highlights some classic works on early medieval hagiography, essential research aids, and useful collections of texts in translation. It is in no way intended to be exhaustive, but should rather act as a gateway into other worlds of scholarship. It is arranged in broad and contestable categories: Buddhist hagiography; studies focusing on women and gender; martyrologies and calendars; Late Antiquity; Insular hagiographies; Merovingian and Carolingian hagiographies; and, finally, broader works and essential resources.

Buddhist Hagiography

Augustine, Jonathan Morris. *Buddhist Hagiography in Early Japan: Images of Compassion in the Gyōki Tradition*. Abingdon: RoutledgeCurzon, 2005.

> For those interested in comparative hagiography, Augustine's study of the changing traditions about the strong-willed eighth-century priest Gyōki is useful for both its conceptual setting and its analysis. Key texts are also translated in an appendix.

Kieschnick, John. *The Eminent Monk: Buddhist Ideals in Medieval Chinese Hagiography*. Honolulu: University of Hawai'i Press, 1997.

A useful book for historians of the early medieval West to get a sense of holy biographies, *mentalités*, and asceticism through a study of three collections, from the sixth, seventh, and tenth centuries.

Studies Focusing on Women and Gender

Coon, Lynda. *Sacred Fictions: Holy Women and Hagiography in Late Antiquity*. Philadelphia: University of Pennsylvania Press, 1997.

A slightly deceptive title: Coon's excellent study examines the ways in which hagiography about women was used to express theological concepts for principally male monastic audiences.

Kitchen, John. *Saints' Lives and the Rhetoric of Gender: Male and Female in Merovingian Hagiography*. Oxford: Oxford University Press, 1998.

Narrower in scope than the title suggests, this book provides a useful analysis of the legends of Radegund and the modern scholarship on the sources.

McNamara, Jo Ann, John Halborg, and E. Gordon Whatley. *Sainted Women of the Dark Ages*. Durham: Duke University Press, 1992.

At the same time a useful collection of female saints' Lives (principally Merovingian) in translation and an important contribution to early medieval gender history.

Talbot, Alice-Mary. *Byzantine Defenders of Images: Eight Saints' Lives in English Translation*. Washington, DC: Dumbarton Oaks Research Library, 1998.

———. *Holy Women of Byzantium: Ten Saints' Lives in English Translation*. Washington, DC: Dumbarton Oaks Research Library, 1996.

These two volumes provide a useful introduction to early Byzantine hagiography, with texts in translation and helpful commentary.

Tsai, Kathryn Ann. *Lives of the Nuns: Biographies of Chinese Buddhist Nuns from the Fourth to Sixth Centuries*. Honolulu: University of Hawai'i Press, 1994.

A full translation of *Biqiuni Zhuan*, a sixth-century collection of biographies about female religious figures in the region around Nanjing.

Martyrologies and Calendars

Borst, Arno. *Die karolingische Kalenderreform*. Hanover: Hahn, 1998.

Borst's overarching thesis—that Charlemagne inaugurated a reform of the calendar in 789—may be doubted as it is presented here, but he provides a wide-ranging and thoroughly researched book that is the essential starting point for studies of the early medieval calendar.

Lifshitz, Felice. *The Name of the Saints: The Martyrology of Jerome and Access to the Sacred in Francia, 627–827*. Notre Dame: University of Notre Dame Press, 2006.

A thought-provoking analysis of the evolution of the martyrology associated with Jerome and some of its implications for the Carolingian cult of saints.

Quentin, Henri. *Les martyrologes historiques du moyen age*. Paris: Gabalda, 1908.

Quentin's study remains an important and instructive effort to disentangle the Carolingian development of historical martyrologies on the basis of the complex and contradictory manuscript evidence.

Rauer, Christine. *The Old English Martyrology*. Cambridge: Brewer, 2013.

A full edition, translation, and commentary of an important martyrology, making it an essential resource for understanding ninth-century developments.

Late Antiquity

Brown, Peter. *Society and the Holy in Late Antiquity*. London: Faber & Faber, 1982.

A collection of Brown's pioneering early essays, including his seminal studies of Syrian holy men and relics in the age of Gregory of Tours.

Dal Santo, Matthew. *Debating the Saints' Cult in the Age of Gregory the Great*. Oxford: Oxford University Press, 2012.

A useful case study that uses the *Dialogues* of Gregory the Great (d. 604) to examine different approaches to cults in the Latin West and Greek East.

Everett, Nicholas. *Patron Saints of Early Medieval Italy, c. 350–800*. Toronto: Toronto University Press, 2017.

This volume provides ten biographies of Italian saints from Late Antiquity with discussion of their historical and literary significance. Most texts are much later than the saints they are about, which makes for some interesting reflection on legend and history.

Fear, Andrew. *Lives of the Visigothic Fathers*. Liverpool: Liverpool University Press, 1997.

Translations of key hagiographic texts from Visigoth Spain, with commentary.

Grig, Lucy. *Making Martyrs in Late Antiquity*. London: Duckworth, 2004.

A stimulating study of the representation of martyrs in narrative and image in the Late Antique West, illuminating the sophisticated use and meaning of such stories.

Harvey, Susan Ashbrook. *Asceticism and Society in Crisis: John of Ephesus and the Lives of the Eastern Saints*. Berkeley: University of California Press, 1990.

A careful analysis and contextualization of an important sixth-century Syriac text, examining some of its implications for understanding more of the politics and culture of the Late Antique East.

Krueger, Derek. *Symeon the Holy Fool: Leontius's Life and the Late Antique City*. Berkeley: University of California Press, 1996.

A study of the urban phenomenon of saints pretending to be fools, with useful translation and commentary of a key Greek text.

——. *Writing and Holiness: The Practice of Authorship in the Early Christian East*. Philadelphia: University of Pennsylvania Press, 2004.

An examination of the social and theological aspects of writing about holiness that helps to focus on the production of hagiography.

Lapidge, Michael. *The Roman Martyrs*. Oxford: Oxford University Press, 2018.

An important collection of early martyrs' stories in translation, highlighting issues of religious conflict and legal process. Lapidge has made many other important contributions to the study of hagiography with editions and translations of neglected texts.

Rapp, Claudia. https://univie.academia.edu/ClaudiaRapp.

Brings together copies of Rapp's important articles on many aspects of Byzantine hagiography.

Stancliffe, Clare. *St Martin and his Hagiographer: History and Miracle in Sulpicius Severus*. Oxford: Clarendon Press, 1983.

A meticulous study of a single hagiography that offers both a historical reconstruction of Martin's career and an assessment of Sulpicius within the thoughtworlds of the fourth century.

Insular Hagiographies

Herbert, Máire. *Iona, Kells and Derry: The History and Hagiography of the Monastic Familia of Columba*. Oxford: Oxford University Press, 1988.

A classic study of the role of hagiography in the formation of a monastic network, focusing on the stories and activities of St. Columba and his heirs.

Rollason, David. *Saints and Relics in Anglo-Saxon England*. Oxford: Blackwell, 1989.

A good overview of the sources for Anglo-Saxon cults with much on hagiography, aimed (still radically in the 1980s) at illustrating the social, political, and ecclesiastical history of early England.

Sharpe, Richard. *Medieval Irish Saints' Lives: An Introduction to Vitae Sanctorum Hiberniae*. Oxford: Clarendon, 1991.

An important—and still controversial—technical analysis of early Irish saints' Lives, in which Sharpe argues that one particular cluster edited by Charles Plummer, later re-edited by W. W. Heist, is from the eighth and ninth centuries.

Merovingian and Carolingian Hagiographies

Egmond, Wolfert van. *Conversing with the Saints: Communication in Pre-Carolingian Hagiography from Auxerre*. Turnhout: Brepols, 2006.

A focused and careful study of the developments of hagiographical traditions in a single centre in the early medieval West.

Fouracre, Paul, and Richard Gerberding. *Late Merovingian France: History and Hagiography, 640–720*. Manchester: Manchester University Press, 1996.

Translations of key hagiographic texts from Merovingian Gaul, alongside two chronicles to help make sense of them, with excellent commentary that helps to open up study of the seventh century.

Goullet, Monique. *Écriture et réécriture hagiographiques: essai sur les réécritures de Vies de saints dans l'Occident latin medieval (VIIIe–XIIIe siècle)*. Turnhout: Brepols, 2005.

A technical philological handbook for understanding the processes involved in rewriting Latin saints' Lives, by a leading scholar involved in the SHG project.

Graus, František. *Volk, Herrschaft und Heiliger im Reich der Merowinger. Studien zur Hagiographie der Merowingerzeit.* Prague: Nakladatelství Československé akademie ved, 1965.

In some senses the first "modern" study of hagiography, in which Graus studied the ideals within Merovingian hagiography in order to understand better the society that produced the texts.

Head, Thomas. *Hagiography and the Cult of Saints: The Diocese of Orléans 800–1200.* Cambridge: Cambridge University Press, 1990.

The golden example of how to study the evolution of hagiographical traditions in a centre, giving insight to the social, political, and intellectual motors for change in those traditions.

Heinzelmann, Martin, Monique Goullet, and Christiane Veyrard-Cosme, eds. *L'hagiographie mérovingienne à travers ses réécritures*. Ostfildern: Thorbecke, 2010.

An invaluable resource, with important essays on language, manuscripts, and rewriting Merovingian saints' Lives. It also includes Martin Heinzelmann's important "panorama," surveying all knownhagiographies from the Merovingian world.

Kreiner, Jamie. *The Social Life of Hagiography in the Merovingian Kingdom*. Cambridge: Cambridge University Press, 2014.

A conceptually wide-ranging study of hagiography as part of political and moral discourse in Gaul, principally in the seventh century.

Neil, Bronwen. *Seventh-Century Popes and Martyrs: The Political Hagiography of Anastasius Bibliothecarius*. Turnhout: Brepols, 2006.

A study that helps to open up the neglected but significant work of translators of hagiography, in this case how Anastasius Bibliothecarius in the ninth century used the stories of Pope Martin I (d. 655) and Maximus the Confessor (d. 662) to make political commentary on his own time. Neil includes editions and translations of the key texts.

Poulin, Joseph-Claude. *L'idéal de sainteté dans l'Aquitaine carolingienne (750–950)*. Québec: Presses de l'Université Laval, 1975.

A study that emphases the conservative but distinctive nature of hagiography in Carolingian Aquitaine through both literary and sociological lenses, providing a useful case study for comparative projects.

Raaijmakers, Janneke. *The Making of the Monastic Community of Fulda*. Cambridge: Cambridge University Press, 2012.

While not a book *about* hagiography, Raaijmakers' study provides a lesson in how to read hagiography as part of a the changing concerns of an institution in serial crisis.

Röckelein, Hedwig. *Reliquientranslationen nach Sachen im 9. Jahurhundert: über Kommunikation, Mobilität und Öffentlichkeit im Frühmittelalter.* Stuttgart: Jan Thorbecke, 2002.

A good example of using hagiographical texts for social history—in this case, using accounts of Saxon relic translations to explore social connections, routes of communication, and ritual.

Smith, Julia. "The Problem of Female Sanctity in Carolingian Europe c. 780–920." *Past & Present* 146 (1995): 3–37.

Julia Smith has written some of the most perceptive essays on Western saints' cults and hagiography. For the purposes of the present book, this classic article is a good place to start with her work, as it explores the intersections of hagiography, society, and constructions of gender.

Taylor, Anna. *Epic Lives and Monasticism in the Middle Ages, 800–1050*. Cambridge: Cambridge University Press, 2013.

A thoughtful examination of neglected poetic *vitae* and their developing didactic functions.

Van Acker, Marieke. *Ut quique rustici et inlitterari hec audierint intellegant: hagiographie et communication verticale au temps des Mérovingiens (VIIe–VIIIe siècles)*. Turnhout: Brepols, 2007.

A detailed technical exploration of the changes in the Latin language that led to Romance, using the evidence of hagiographies and their use—the kind of analysis that helps us to move beyond assessments of Merovingian Latin as "ungrammatical" and "barbaric."

Van Dam, Raymond. *Saints and their Cults in Late Antique Gaul*. Princeton: Princeton University Press, 1993.

A collection of miracle stories in translation, mostly by Gregory of Tours (d. 594), with four introductory essays intended to provide sketches of the social value of such stories while challenging Peter Brown's anachronistic and generalizing uses of the same material.

Van Uytfanghe, Marc. *Stylisation biblique et condition humaine dans l'hagiographie mérovingienne (600–750)*. Brussels: Paleis der Academië, 1987.

A detailed and systematic study of the biblical and patristic influence on Merovingian writers, helping to rescue further the reputation of the authors as sophisticated and intellectually engaged writers.

Wood, Ian. *The Missionary Life: Saints and the Evangelisation of Europe 400–1050*. Harlow: Routledge, 2001.

An exemplary study of hagiographical narratives as textual arguments, each with their own social logic, using examples of early medieval accounts of mission.

Broader Works and Essential Resources

Bartlett, Robert. *Why Can the Dead do Such Great Things? Saints and Worshippers from the Martyrs to the Reformation*. Princeton: Princeton University Press, 2013.

A well-crafted account of medieval sanctity in its many forms, with the merits of being geographically and chronologically broad in scope.

Berschin, Walter. *Biographie und Epochenstil im lateinischen Mittelalter*. 5 vols. Stuttgart: Hiersemann, 1988–2001.

A magisterial exploration of the evolution of biographical forms in medieval Latin, with much to say about the role of hagiography.

Brown, Peter. *The Rise of Western Christendom*. 3rd ed. Oxford: Wiley-Blackwell, 2013.

A highly influential evocation of changing patterns of belief in the transformation from Roman worlds to medieval Christendoms, often drawing on hagiographical vignettes.

Delehaye, Hippolyte. *Les légendes hagiographiques*. Brussels: Société des Bollandistes, 1905. Translated by Donald Attwater. *The Legends of the Saints*. 4th ed. Dublin: Four Courts Press, 1998.

Over a century old, and still the standard useful place to start when learning about source criticism and hagiographies.

Efthymiadis, Stephanos, ed. *Ashgate Research Companion to Byzantine Hagiography*. 2 vols. Farnham: Ashgate, 2011–14.

An essential collection of essays surveying core themes and issues in Byzantine hagiography, with many lessons for non-Byzantinists.

Geary, Patrick. *Living with the Dead in the Middle Ages*. Ithaca: Cornell University Press, 1994.

A collection of essays, most focusing on elements of hagiography and relic cults, and building on his 1978 study of relic translations, *Furta Sacra*.

Heffernan, Thomas J. *Sacred Biography: Saints and their Biographers in the Middle Ages*. Oxford: Oxford University Press, 1988.

A notable study that sought to understand "the mentality of the Middle Ages" through an avowedly literary, almost postmodern and wide-ranging reading of "sacred biographies"—a term employed as part of an effort to step away from the baggage of the term "hagiography."

Heinzelmann, Martin. *Translationsberichte und andere Quellen des Reliquienkultes*. Turnhout: Brepols, 1979.

A useful short introduction to relic cults and the sources for them.

Howard-Johnston, James and Paul Anthony Hayward, eds. *The Cult of Saints in Late Antiquity and the Early Middle Ages*. Oxford: Oxford University Press, 1999.

A collection of essays reflecting on Peter Brown's work on saints, many touching on important issues within Latin, Greek, and Syriac hagiography.

Philippart, Guy, ed. *Hagiographies*. 6 vols. Turnhout: Brepols, 1994–present.

An invaluable collaborative attempt to establish "an international history of the Latin and vernacular hagiographical literature in the West from its origins to 1550," with essays from leading experts on different areas and periods.

——. *Les légendiers latins et autres manuscrits hagiographiques*. Turnhout: Brepols, 1977.

A short introduction to the manuscript sources for studying early medieval hagiography.

Poulin, Joseph-Claude. "Les *Libelli* dans l'edition hagiographique avant le XIIe siècle." In *Livrets, Collections et Textes. Études sur la tradition hagiographique latin*, edited by Martin Heinzelmann, 15–194. Ostfildern: Jan Thorbecke, 2006.

An essential guide to early hagiographies preserved (on the whole) by themselves in early manuscripts.

Vauchez, André. *La sainteté en Occident aux derniers siècles du Moyen Age d'après les process de canonisation et les documents hagiographiques*. Rome: École Française de Rome, 1979. Translated by Jean Birrell as *Sainthood in the Later Middle Ages*. Cambridge: Cambridge University Press, 1997.

After Graus's work, one of the foundational efforts to use hagiography for social history. Although it is focused on the later Middle Ages, Vauchez's study contains useful reflections on the earlier period and the changing nature of sanctity over time.